W9-AHA-628

BUILD IT WITH
BOXES

By Joan Irvine
Illustrated by Linda Hendry

Morrow Junior Books
New York

First published in Canada in 1991 by Kids Can Press, 585½ Bloor
Street West, Toronto, Ontario, Canada   M6G 1K5

Printed in the United States of America.

1 2 3 4 5 6 7 8 9 10

Library of Congress Cataloging-in-Publication Data
Irvine, Joan, 1951–
  [Make it with boxes]
  Build it with boxes / Joan Irvine ; illustrated by Linda Hendry.
    p. cm.
  Originally published: Make it with boxes. Toronto : Kids Can
Press, c1991.
    Summary: Explains how to make boxes and box creations, including
a fish, dragon, camera, airplane, and tropical rain forest.
    ISBN 0-688-12081-4 (trade)—ISBN 0-688-11524-1 (library)
    1. Box craft—Juvenile literature. [1. Box craft.
  2. Handicraft.] I. Hendry, Linda, ill. II. Title.
  TT870.5.I78 1993   745.54—dc20   91-45589 CIP AC

Contents

*I would like to dedicate this book to the
Big Bay Box Club, and to my family,
Steven, Elly and Seth.*

Acknowledgements

Many people contributed ideas and creative energy to this book. I would like to thank a group of children ages six to twelve who call themselves The Big Bay Box Club. During the summer of 1989, they made many box creations, wrote a five-act play using the boxes and performed the drama in front of an audience. The members of the club were Elly Irvine, Seth Irvine, Margaret Loney, Laura Burns, Bethany Martin, Johanna Martin, Aaron Schneider, Isaac Schneider, Erin Scheel and Angie Wray.

I would also like to thank my Grade 5 class 1989/90 at Keppel-Sarawak School, Owen Sound, Canada, for their ideas and enthusiasm.

Many thanks to my own children and husband, who were very supportive and patient during the writing of this book.

A great thank you goes to my wonderful editors. My first editor, Val Wyatt, helped in the creative development of the manuscript. My second editor, Elizabeth MacLeod, and production editor, Ronda Arab, assisted me in polishing and organizing the final manuscript. Finally, I would like to acknowledge the ever-supportive team at Kids Can Press, especially Valerie Hussey and Ricky Englander.

Credits go to the following people for their ideas:

Ann Schneider — airplane
Stewart Robertson — elephant mask
Mark Cruikshank — large standing
    puppets
Tom Vanden Berg — ideas for shadow
    puppets
Margaret Loney and Elly Irvine — mini-
    golf activities

I would also like to thank Kodak for their permission to use and adapt "How to Make and Use a Pinhole Camera."

Introduction

If you have a large cardboard box, you can make a puppet stage, a fort or a giant dragon. With small to medium-sized boxes, you can create costumes, puppets, dioramas and many other exciting projects. You can even make your own boxes and use them as baskets, as jewellery cases or as decorations. This book will give you lots of ideas for making boxes and making things with boxes.

Boxes have been around for a long time. Did you know that in the 19th century North Americans and Europeans used wooden boxes for storing household items? They made Bible boxes, spice boxes, candle boxes and boxes for bread dough. Today, boxes are usually made of paper and are found everywhere. You probably have some in your kitchen cupboards and closets. If you don't have any empty boxes, ask your local stores for some.

In this book, there are projects that use two different kinds of boxes. One type is a heavy, rigid cardboard box, such as a box holding a new refrigerator. The other is a light paper box, such as a tissue box or cereal box. Both types are very different.

If you split open the sides of a heavy cardboard box, you will find the paper is put together like a sandwich. The layers are made up of flat and corrugated board glued together. It's the corrugations that make the box so strong. You can find heavy cardboard boxes in supermarkets, furniture stores and appliance stores.

The lighter boxes are called cartons in the paper industry. Cartons are stamped out of a piece of paper board.

Start saving boxes now and you will have many hours of fun making the projects in this book.

Materials

To make your boxes or work with them, you will need the following materials.

Boxes See the *Materials* section for each activity for the type of box you need.

Paper Use construction paper, gift wrap, tissue paper, wallpaper or other paper to make or cover boxes.

Cutting Blade When cutting light cardboard, you can use an Olfa touch knife. To cut thick cardboard, a heavy cutting blade, such as a utility knife, is useful. Have an adult do the cutting for you. **When you see this symbol, it means you need an adult to help you.** △!

Scissors Check with an adult before using any scissors. A sharp, heavy pair can be used to cut many boxes. Remember to use all cutting equipment with care.

Glue When adding paper decorations, use a glue stick or white glue. Use white glue when gluing heavier things together.

Paint Choose a safe, non-toxic paint, such as tempera. Paint will not stick to boxes that have a waxed coating.

Tape Clear tape can be used to secure light paper. With larger or heavier projects, you should use masking tape.

Stapler When attaching light pieces of cardboard, carefully use a stapler.

Brass Fasteners These are available at stationery or business supply stores.

Ruler Use a ruler for making any measurements. A ruler is especially necessary when making your own boxes.

Twist-ties Twist-ties can be used to strengthen moving parts. They can also be used to join boxes together.

String Boxes can be joined together with heavy string. Punch small holes in the boxes and lace them together.

Fabrics, feathers, ribbon, buttons, sequins, glitter and magazines can be used to decorate your boxes.

Tips
General Tips

- If you are using a utility knife to cut large boxes, ask an adult to do the cutting for you.

- It is often difficult to join large boxes together. One good method is to punch small holes in boxes where you want to join them and attach them together with string, pipe cleaners or large twist-ties.

- Be neat and careful when you work. Spread newspapers under painting projects. Do any cutting carefully so you don't damage your work space. Large projects are easier to do outside or in a garage.

- You can usually cover mistakes with paper decorations. A decorative trim or a strip of paper can cover the rough edges of a box. Dioramas can be trimmed with strips of paper.

- If you are painting a large cardboard box, remove tape or labels first if possible.

- Paint will not stick to tape or coated paper. It is easier to cover some boxes, such as cereal boxes or milk cartons, with paper instead of painting them.

Tips for Folding and Scoring

You will need to fold and score paper to make your own paper boxes. To make a straight fold on heavy paper, *score* the paper first. Scoring means making a crease on your paper along the line to be folded. Lay a metal ruler close to the line to be folded. Then carefully run the blunt end of a pair of scissors or a ball-point pen that's run out of ink along the fold line. When you fold your paper, press firmly.

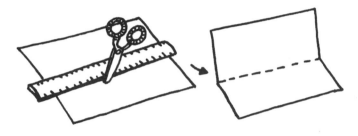

Tips for Measuring

All measurements are given in both metric and imperial systems. Measurements differ slightly from system to system.

Symbols and Definitions

The following symbols and definitions will be useful to you when you use this book.

- Flap: a piece of paper or cardboard that hangs loose.

- Tab: a paper insert or area that can be glued.

- Spring: a folded device that makes an object pop up.

- Fold line   – – – – – – – –

- Cut line   ————————

- Glue

- Tape

Recycle—Be Environmentally Friendly

You will be recycling boxes, cartons and other household objects when you make the projects in this book. Look around your home for other objects that would normally be thrown away. Lids, string, gift wrap, fabric, plastic inserts in boxes and artificial flowers can find a new life in one of your box activities.

With some projects, you may be able to recycle the boxes once again. If you make a costume, you can use the mask later as a room decoration. Large boxes used in costumes can be used as toy boxes or for storing other things.

Cutting and Folding Ideas

By adding curled, folded or pierced paper to your boxes, you can make more interesting projects.

Paper curling: You can curl paper by pulling it tightly over the edge of a scissor blade. Paper curls can make hair on puppets or decorations in dioramas.

Accordion folding: Fold paper back and forth to create accordion folds. Accordion-folded blue paper makes wavy water in dioramas.

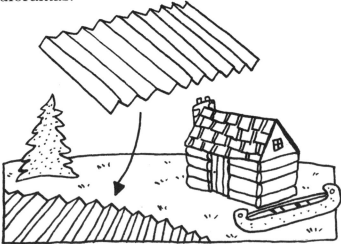

Piercing: You can pierce a box or paper with a sharp object such as a compass or with a paper-punch. If you are making a closed diorama with a peep-hole, pierced holes in the lid can add interesting lighting to the scene.

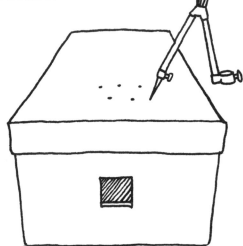

Slitting: By slitting paper or cartons with a cutting blade or sharp scissors and then folding back the cut paper, you can create many shapes.

Decorating Tips for Boxes

Spattering: By dipping an old toothbrush into paint and then flicking it with your finger, you can spatter a box or paper with paint.

Print making: By dipping pieces of sponge, pieces of vegetables or found objects into paint and then pressing them onto boxes or paper, you can make interesting prints.

Bubble prints: Pour equal amounts of liquid detergent and water into an old cup. Add several drops of food colouring and blow into the mixture with a straw. When the bubbles rise over the surface of the cup, gently lower a piece of paper onto the bubbles. Do this several times and you will have a bubble print.

Making Shapes to Add to Your Boxes

Horns or cones: Roll part of a circle and secure it with tape.

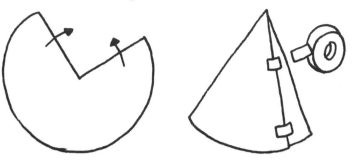

Cylinder: Roll a rectangular piece of paper and secure it with tape or glue.

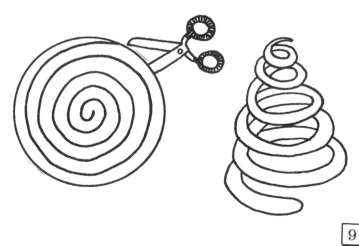

Spirals: Cut a spiral out of a circle. Spirals make interesting hair on box masks.

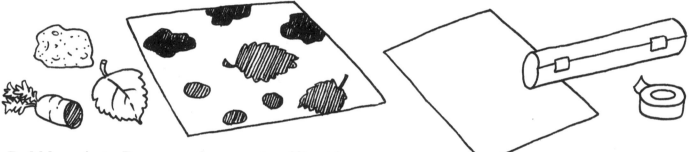

Part One Make Your Own Boxes

There are a number of ways you can make your own boxes. You can:

- use geometric shapes
- use a pattern
- fold paper (origami)

The boxes in this chapter can be used to:

- hold gifts
- hold dry food or candies
- store jewellery
- keep collections such as cards, coins or stickers
- make ornaments

To make the boxes in this chapter, you will need scissors, a ruler, heavy paper and, in some cases, tape. Remember to use heavy paper or light bristol board if you are going to put heavy objects into your box.

When your box is completed, try adding different kinds of decoration. You can glue on curled paper, ribbons, stickers or glitter. Use your imagination to create an interesting box.

After you have learned how to make a variety of boxes, you can combine them to make your own "Geometric World." See the end of the chapter for some great ideas. Have fun with your box making!

Shape a Box

By shifting or moving these shapes around and tracing them, you can make a pattern for a fold-up box. After you have followed several ideas in this book, you can design your own boxes.

To Make the Shapes

Here are the shapes you'll need to make fold-up boxes. To make small boxes out of a single sheet of 22 cm x 28 cm (8½ in. x 11 in.) paper, trace the small shapes. For larger boxes, trace the big shapes. (You'll need larger pieces of paper, such as gift wrap.)

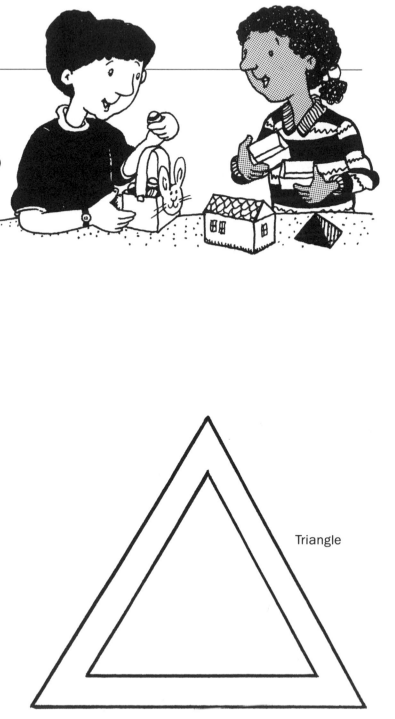

Parallelogram

Triangle

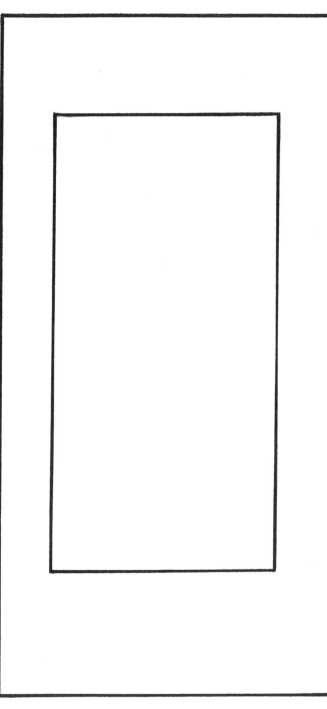

Rectangle

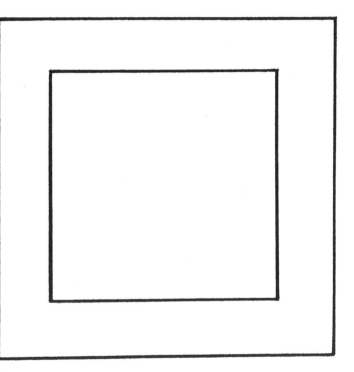

Square

Trace the shapes onto white paper, then carefully cut them out.

Did you know that the rectangle is made by joining two squares? The parallelogram is made by joining two triangles.

To make sturdier patterns, glue the shapes to bristol board and cut them out.

Now that you have the four basic shapes, you're ready to make many kinds of boxes.

See the ideas on the following pages.

Make a Small Box

Materials

geometric shapes from pages 12 and 13
a piece of paper or bristol board — 22 cm x
   28 cm (8½ in. x 11 in.) (if you are using
   the small geometric shapes) or larger
   paper (if you are using the big shapes)
Also: scissors, clear tape (or glue or stapler),
   pencil, ruler

Here is your box pattern. Steps 1 to 4 tell you how to draw it.

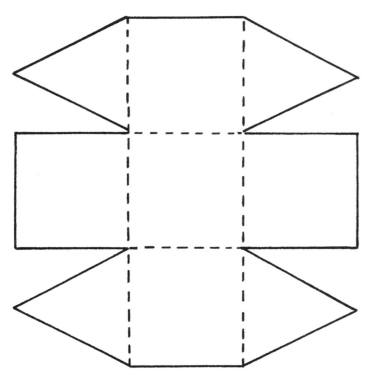

1 Lay the square shape in the middle of your paper and trace around it with a pencil.

2 Then place the square shape immediately beside the square that you have drawn and carefully trace around it.

3 Follow the pattern below and add the other squares and triangles in the same way. Cut around the outside of your shape.

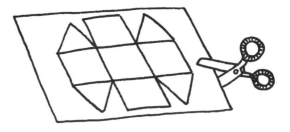

4 *Score* the dotted lines on the pattern. See page 7 about scoring.

5 Fold the square sides upwards first. Then fold in the triangular ends. Tape, staple or glue the triangle ends of the box to the rest of the box. Now you have a small box.

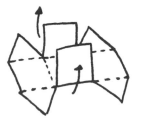

More Small Boxes

Gift Basket

Make your box into a basket by adding a handle to it. Cut a strip of paper 28 cm x 2.5 cm (11 in. x 1 in.) and fasten it to the sides of the box using staples or tape.

Easter Basket

Add a handle to the box (see left). Draw, colour and cut out a rabbit's head and glue it to one end of the box. Glue a pom-pom tail to the other end of the box.

Party Candy Holder

Draw, colour and cut out flowers. Glue them to the outside edge of the box. Put candies inside the box and place one in front of each party guest!

Box with a Lid

If you make two identical boxes, you can fit one inside the other.

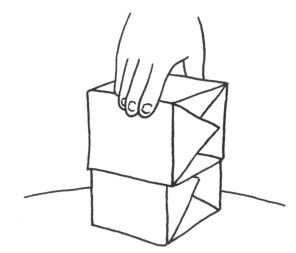

More Ideas Using Geometric Shapes

By tracing and cutting out the basic geometric shapes, you can make these boxes and objects.

Use the geometric shapes, paper, a ruler, a pair of scissors and glue or tape. Follow the patterns carefully.

Rectangular Box

Use the rectangle, square and triangle shapes. Fold the sides and ends up, overlap the triangular ends and fasten them with tape or glue. If you make two boxes, you can fit one inside the other to form a lid.

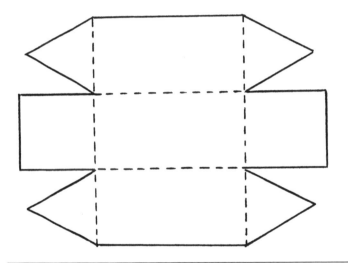

Triangular Prism

Use a square and a triangle shape. You will have to add tabs to the pattern as shown, to make gluing your prism easier. If you make two prisms, you can glue them together to make a hanging ornament! Attach a string to the top of the ornament.

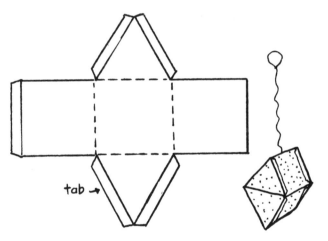

tab →

Pyramid

You will need a square and a triangle shape to make a pyramid. The four triangles bordering the square are the sides of your pyramid and the other triangles fold inside to make gluing easy. Glue two pyramids together to create a hanging ornament. Add string to the top of the ornament to hang it.

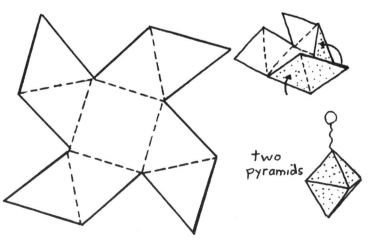

two pyramids

House-shaped Box

1 Use a large piece of paper that is at least 35 cm x 30 cm (14 in. x 12 in.). Use the small rectangle, square and triangle shapes. (This is basically a rectangular box with a roof.) Remember to add tabs to the pattern, then cut it out.

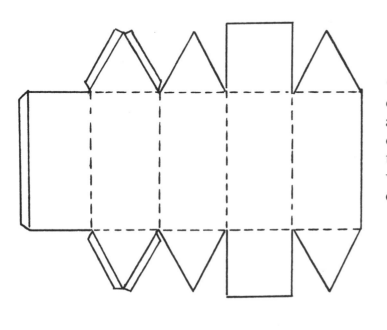

2 Fold the bottom first. Glue or tape the triangular ends to make a box.

3 Fold the roof over. Glue or tape the two tabs inside the triangular ends to create a roof shape. If you wish to make this a box that opens, do not glue the long tab or the bottom side tabs of the roof. Tuck these tabs inside the bottom area of the house when it is in a closed position. If you want a closed house shape, glue all tabs in place.

Diamond-shaped Box

1 You will need a large piece of paper, at least 35 cm x 30 cm (14 in. x 12 in.). To make this box, use the small rectangle and parallelogram shapes. Remember to add tabs before cutting it out.

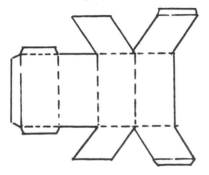

2 When folding the box, glue or tape the side tabs first and then secure the bottom. Close the flaps at the top of the box last.

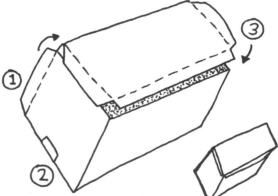

Make Boxes from Cards

Ever wondered what to do with old
Christmas, Hanukkah or birthday cards?
You can make sturdy little boxes from them.
Then you can use the boxes to hold
jewellery, stickers or small objects.

Materials

a card with a colourful pattern (and one that
   you can cut up!)
Also: scissors, glue (optional), pencil

1 To make the lid, cut the card in half.
Put one half aside.

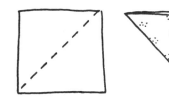

2 Make the other half card into a square
by folding the top left corner of the card
diagonally to *exactly* meet the right side of
the card. Press the fold firmly. Cut off the
remaining strip below the folded section.
Repeat this with the other half card.

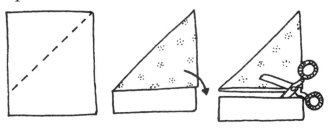

3 Open the more colourful square and
place it coloured side down. Fold it
along the other diagonal, so that you have
two fold lines. Mark the centre of the square
with a dot.

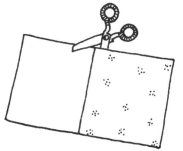

4 Fold each corner of the square to the
centre dot.

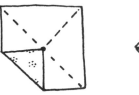

5 Fold the top half of the square towards
the centre. Fold the bottom half to the
centre. Press both folds firmly then open
them again.

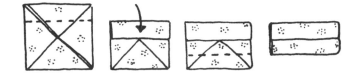

6 Now fold the sides towards the centre.

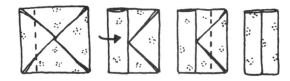

18

7 Open the whole square of paper so it's completely flat. With a pencil, lightly mark the fold lines of the middle square you just made.

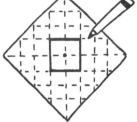

8 Starting at each corner of the middle square, mark the fold lines that lead to the edge of the paper. Cut these four lines into each corner of the middle square.

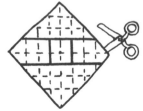

9 Fold the corners marked with an * in the diagram to the centre dot.

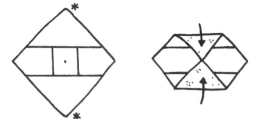

10 Fold the long sides up.

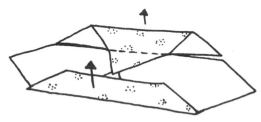

11 Fold the ends of the long sides into the middle to form the sides of the box.

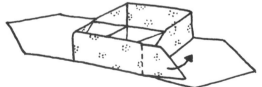

12 Bring the end flaps up and over the sides so the tips meet in the centre of the bottom. If you wish, put a dab of glue under the tips.

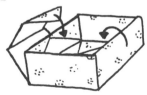

13 *Optional* Cut 2 small notches in the side areas of the lid. This makes the box easier to open.

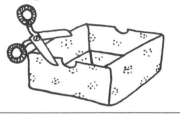

14 To make the bottom of the box, make another box in the same way using the other half of your card. Fit the two together.

Variation

You can use old magazine pages or magazine covers to make boxes in the same way. Make sure that each page is trimmed and square before using it.

Make an Origami Box

Try this traditional origami idea to make a small box. It's different from the box you just made because it uses no cutting or gluing. All you need is a piece of origami paper or a square piece of paper.

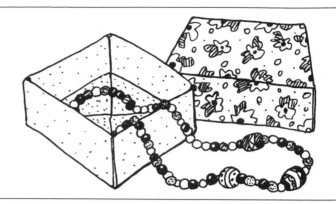

1 Fold a square of paper into quarters.

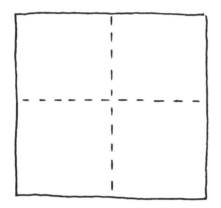

2 Fold each corner into the centre.

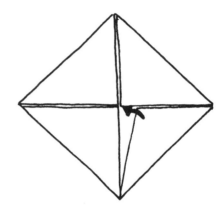

3 Fold two opposite sides into the middle, then unfold them.

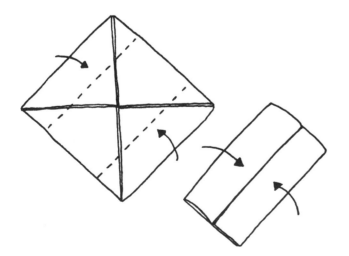

4 Fold the other opposite two sides into the middle and then unfold them.

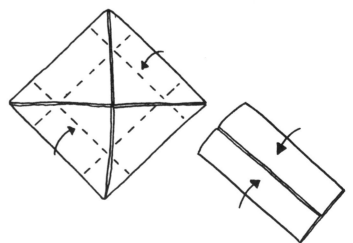

5 Open out two opposite ends.

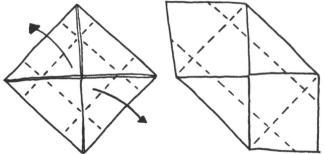

6 Fold the two folded sides up to form two of the sides of your box.

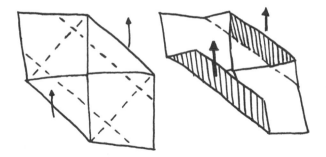

7 Here comes the tricky part! Make one end of your box by folding one tip upwards, tucking in the folds at the sides to form corners.

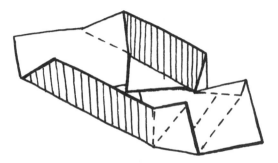

8 Pull the tip up and over the edge, into the centre of the box. Repeat with the other end of the box.

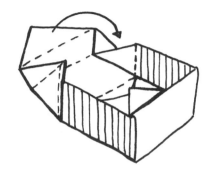

9 If you make two boxes, you can fit one into the other to make a lidded box.

Variation

Do you want to give a tiny present in an interesting way? Make lidded boxes in various sizes and put your gift in the smallest one. Then put that box in the next smallest box. Continue doing this until all the boxes are inside the largest box.

Fantastic Worlds

Make your own fantastic geometric world
by combining geometric pieces and boxes
and gluing them onto a cardboard base.
Here are some ideas:

Tropical Beach Scene

accordion fold
blue paper
to make
water

grass glued on roof

tissue paper
leaves

toilet paper
rolls for
trunks

glue on
sand

Winter Village Scene

cotton balls
for snow

roll green paper into
cones to make
Christmas trees

glue on
beads for
Christmas
lights

Pioneer Scene

Plasticine makes a good base for trees, fence posts, etc.

Construction Site

Popsicle stick lumber

City Street

Part Two **Surprise in a Box**

Imagine making a magical tropical world in the moonlight, or making a television set that transforms into a robot. In this chapter, you will make things inside boxes that will surprise and astound your friends.

Tips

- Recycle! Use lids from bottles, or plastic inserts from chocolate boxes for decorating.

- Collect pictures from magazines or interesting objects to add to your boxes. Save ribbon, lace, buttons, sequins or artificial flowers.

- Often grocery stores throw away interesting display boxes or boxes cut on an angle. Ask if you can have them.

- Check shoe stores for extra shoe boxes.

- Use interesting lighting or tape-recorded music to add further atmosphere to your scenes.

- Make a diorama to go with a school project. It will really bring your topic to life.

Make a Hungry Fish

Materials

a small box, such as a shoe box
gift wrap, coloured paper, foil or paint
  (and paint brush)
4 strips of heavy bristol board, each 10 cm
  x 1.5 cm (4 in. x ½ in.)
4 brass fasteners
2 strips of heavy bristol board, each 4 cm x
  1.5 cm (1½ in. x ½ in.) (for reinforcement)
a 7 cm x 7 cm (2¾ in. x 2¾ in.) square from
  panty hose or an old nylon stocking,
  preferably coloured
a small piece of heavy white paper
paper in an assortment of colours
Also: scissors, clear tape, glue

1 Cover the outside of your box with either coloured paper, foil or paint. Cover the inside of the box with blue paper or paint so that it looks like water.

2 With the pointed scissors, make a hole in the middle of each of the four long strips of bristol board. Pair the strips so the holes are on top of each other and put a brass fastener through the middle of each pair.

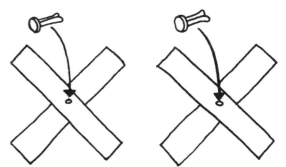

3 Make holes and insert brass fasteners to attach the crossed strips to each other, as shown. Don't bend the brass fasteners open yet.

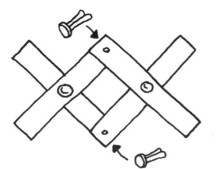

4 Reinforce a pair of long strips by taping a short strip to the end of each one, as shown.

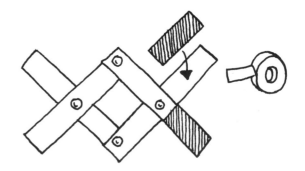

5 Turn your structure over and pull the four corners of the nylon square over the four brass fasteners, piercing the material. This covers the open hole between the four strips. Open the brass fasteners. Trim off any excess material and tape the nylon to the strips.

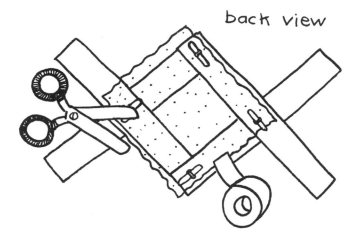

back view

6 Cut out five small triangular teeth and glue them to the strips that are *not* reinforced.

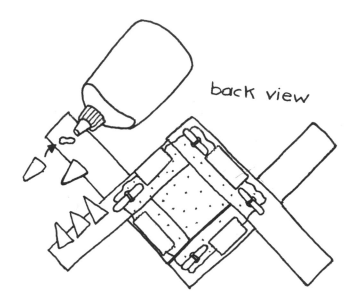

back view

7 Cut out 18 different coloured scales that are 5 cm (2 in.) long and 2 cm (¾ in.) wide. The scales can be cut from foil, tissue or construction paper.

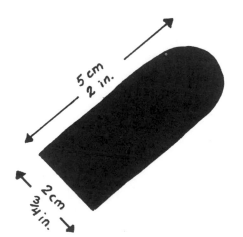

5 cm
2 in.

2 cm
¾ in.

8 Flip your structure to the front again and glue three scales to each strip so that they are overlapping. Do not attach scales to the reinforced strips.

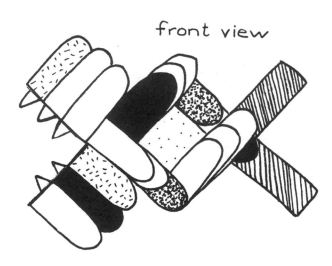

front view

9 Make an eye from tissue paper (or use a small bead). Glue it above the teeth.

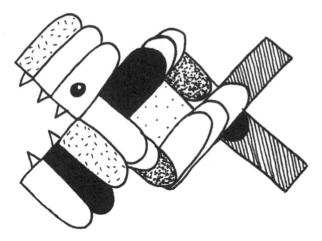

10 Cut a slot 3.5 cm (1½ in.) long in the middle area of the right side of your box. Reinforce the sides of the slot with pieces of tape. Put your fish in the box and slide the tail strips through the slot, as shown.

11 Draw and cut out a little fish. Make a paper tab 8 cm x 2 cm (3¼ in. x ¾ in.) and fold it in half widthwise. Glue the top of the tab to the back of the small fish. Then glue the bottom of the tab to the bottom of the box in front of the hungry fish.

12 Decorate the rest of your scene with ocean creatures. You can make seahorses, starfish and coral from paper. Squeeze the tail of your hungry fish and watch its teeth snap!

Variation

Make a dragon snapping at a knight.

Transform a Television into a Robot

Materials

a heavy cardboard box with flaps — a 28 cm
x 22 cm x 20 cm (11 in. x 8½ in. x 7½ in.)
box works well
a small light box that is smaller than a flap
on your larger box
2 pieces of bristol board that are as *wide*
as a flap on the larger box and as *long*
as the flap length *plus* half the length
tempera or other paint and paint brush
2 long pipe cleaners
stickers and scraps of metallic paper
Optional: buttons, chocolate box insert
Also: scissors, utility knife, clear tape,
masking tape, glue, markers

1 Have an adult cut the two front sides of the larger heavy box as far as the bottom.

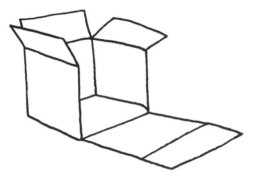

2 Attach the smaller box with tape or glue to the middle edge of the flap of the cut section. This box is the robot's head and *must* sit within the flap.

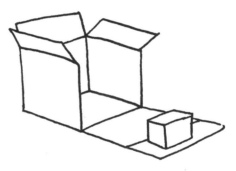

3 To make the robot's arms, place each of the two rectangular pieces of cardboard on either side of the head on the flap and secure with masking tape.

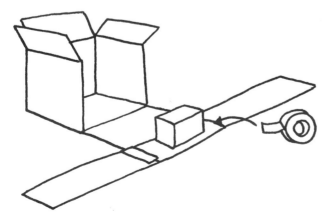

4 Fold in the end of each arm to the point where it attaches to the flap.

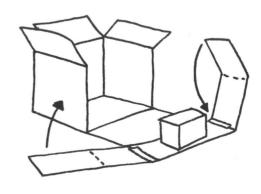

5 To fold the robot into the box, fold its arms together above the head. Fold the head and arms down and forward into the box. (If the arms don't fit, cut and re-fold them.) Lift the other side flaps up while folding the head section into the box. Close the side flaps. You should have a closed box again.

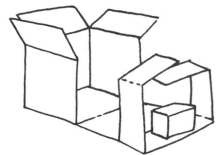

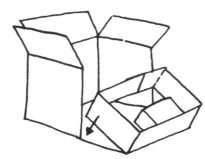

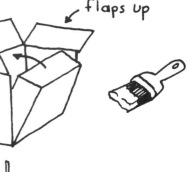

flaps up

6 Paint the entire box structure inside and outside, with one colour. Wait until the paint is dry before going on to the next stage. (If any of the cardboard can't be painted, cover it with foil.)

7 To make the television set on the outside of the box, draw a screen and control knobs on the cut section that folds out (the robot's chest). Bend a long pipe cleaner in half and tape it to the top of the box for antennae.

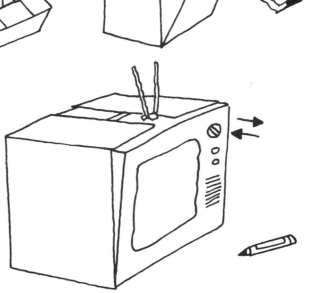

8 To transform your television into a robot:

A. Open the top side flaps and fold the front section down and out, so that the head is facing up. With the head facing you, hold the shoulders and lift the structure up.

B. Bend the bottom of the box, so that the open end is at the back.

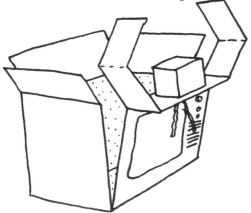

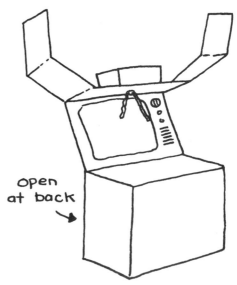

open at back

C. Fold the "hands" inwards and place them on the box in front of the television screen. The hands should support the structure so that it can stand alone.

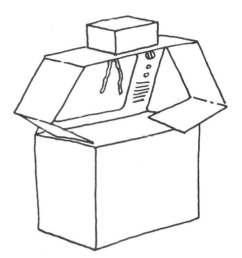

9 Give your robot a face with pipe cleaners and stickers or whatever you like.

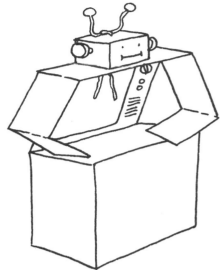

10 You can make another robot face on the other side. The "chest" can be decorated with stickers, buttons and paper clips. The plastic insert used in chocolate boxes makes a great control panel.

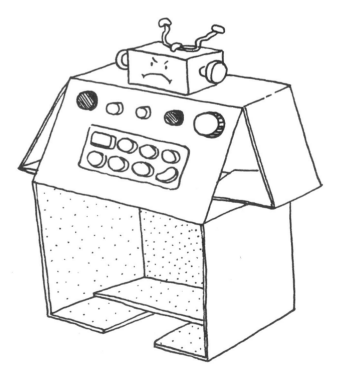

11 To fold up your robot, lift the arms above its head and fold the hands on top of one another. Keep folding the head back and down, until all the sections fold into the box. Lift the side flaps to fold the structure inside. Close the side flaps and you have a television set again!

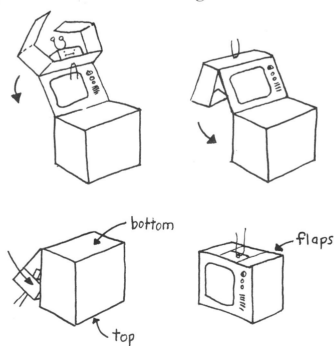

bottom

top

flaps

Pop-ups in a Box

Materials

a small box with a lid, such as a jewellery
    box (or make one, see pages 14 — 21)
a piece of heavy paper, the same size as
    the base of your box
2 strips of heavy paper — 28 cm x 2.5 cm
    (11 in. x 1 in.)
gift wrap (optional)
Also: scissors, glue

1 Draw, colour and cut out a paper heart that can fit into your box. Write or draw a message on your heart or fasten a small present, such as a ring, to the top of it.

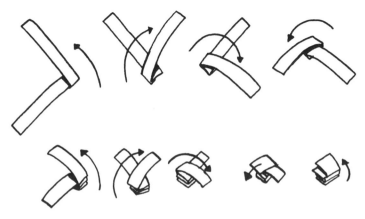

2 To make the pop-up spring, apply glue to the end of one strip of paper. Lay the other strip at right angles to the first strip on the glued area. Allow the glue to dry.

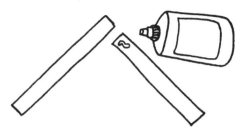

3 Bring the strip on the right side over to the left side and fold the edge. Bring the strip on the bottom up and over the glued area. Bring the strip on the left side over to the right side. Bring the strip on the top down to the bottom area. Continue overlapping the strips until all the paper is folded.

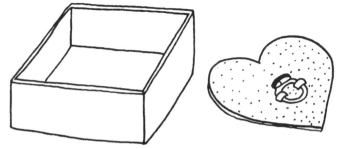

4 Apply glue under the top flap of paper and press the flap down. Cut off any extra paper on each strip.

5 Pull the spring out slightly. Apply glue to one end of the spring and glue it to the back of the heart.

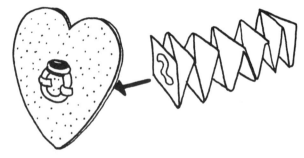

6 Apply glue to the other end of the spring and attach the heart with the spring to the bottom of your small box.

7 Put the lid on your box. If you wish, you can wrap the box with gift wrap. When your friend lifts the lid to the box, the heart will pop up!

Variation:

A spiral spring will work well glued to the lid of your box.

1 Use a piece of heavy paper that is the same size as the base of your box. Round the corners to make a circle, then cut the circle into a spiral.

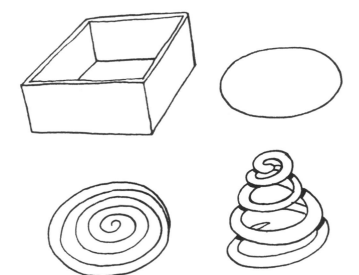

2 Glue the end of the spiral inside the lid of the box. Attach a small heart to the top of the spiral. Put a message on the heart.

3 Put a small present in the bottom of the box!

33

Make a Tropical Rain Forest in the Moonlight

Materials

a shoe box (or any rectangular box) with
  a lid
green paper
small squares of coloured tissue paper
small pieces of coloured paper
green pipe cleaners or twist-ties
a strip of bristol board, 7.5 cm x 2 cm
  (3 in. x ¾ in.)
a small piece of foil
yarn or string
⚠ Also: scissors, Olfa touch knife, clear tape,
  glue

You'll have fun making a rain forest diorama in a box. What is a diorama? It's a scene in a box. When your rain forest scene is finished, you'll be able to hold the box up to a light and see your miniature world through a peep-hole.

1 Remove the lid of the shoe box. Line the inside bottom of the box with green paper and secure it with tape. It is more interesting to use shiny green paper if you can because of the way the light reflects when the box is covered.

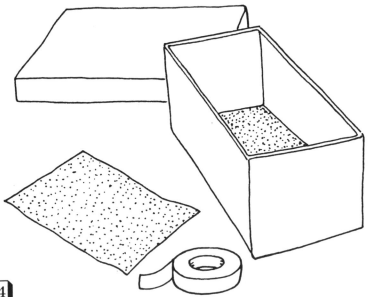

2 Using the scissors, cut a small square hole 2.5 cm x 2.5 cm (1 in. x 1 in.) in the end of your box. This is your peep-hole.

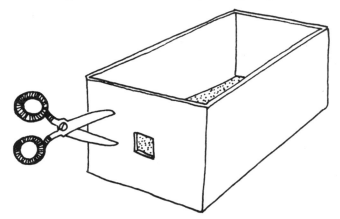

3 Make a larger hole 7.5 cm x 5 cm (3 in. x 2 in.) in the other end of your box.

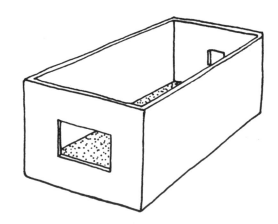

4 Tape or glue a piece of coloured tissue paper 10 cm x 7.5 cm (4 in. x 3 in.) over the larger hole. You may want to experiment with different colours of tissue.

5 To decorate the inside of the box, cut out butterflies, colourful frogs, birds and snakes to glue along the inside walls of your box. You can get ideas from books about the rain forest.

6 For the bottom of your box, you can draw, colour and cut out figures with tabs to fix on the floor with tape or glue. You could make trees, vines and animals such as jaguars.

7 To create action in your box, make two small holes close together in the lid. Insert a looped green pipe cleaner through the two holes on the outside of the lid. On the inside of the lid, twist each end of the pipe cleaner into a circle. You have now created swinging vines. Make a monkey that can hang from the vines. If you move the pipe cleaner from the outside of the lid, the monkey will swing!

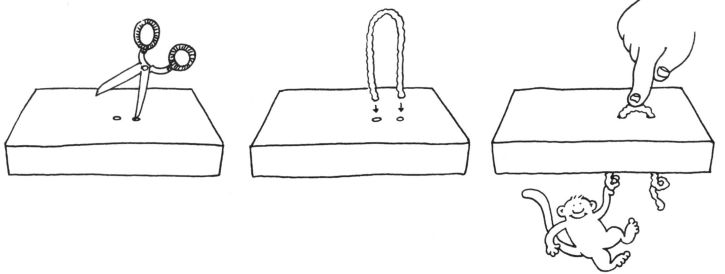

8 To make a sliding moon, make a straight cut across the back area of the lid. Insert a bristol board strip through the slot. Cut out a small round circle of bristol board for a moon and cover it with foil. Secure it to the bottom of the strip with glue.

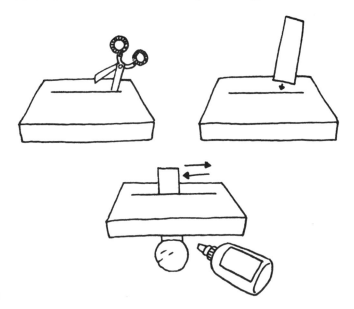

9 To secure the strip in the slot, cut a small piece of bristol board and make a slit in the middle. Slide this piece sideways over the strip at the top of the lid and tape the piece to the strip.

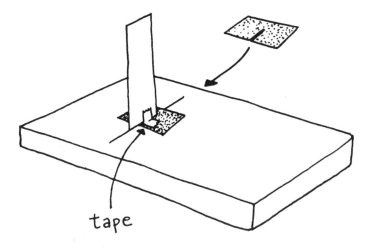

tape

10 To get more light in your box, cut holes in the lid and secure pieces of coloured tissue paper over them.

11 You can tape pieces of yarn and thin strips of tissue paper to the inside of the lid so that they hang down like vines. If you wish, cover or paint the outside of your box. Hold the box up to a light and look through the peep-hole at your rain forest.

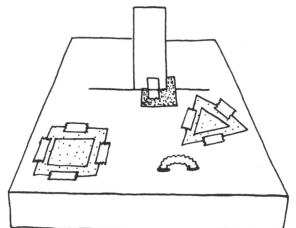

More Dioramas

Have you ever wanted to make a miniature circus, with elephants, flying acrobats and clowns? You can if you make a diorama! If you look at the following ideas, you can build your own miniature world in a box!

Materials

box — a shoe box or a box from a grocery store works well
different kinds of paper
buttons, sequins, ribbon, etc.
brass fasteners (optional)
⚠ Also: scissors, Olfa touch knife (optional), clear tape, glue

What kind of world or scene do you want to create?

Here are some ideas:
Insect World • Circus Scene • Jungle • Underwater World • Room in a Haunted House • Mountain Scene • Mad Monster Scene • Picnic in a Forest • Lunar Landscape • Underground Scene • City Street

There are many ways of preparing boxes for dioramas.

You can cut the flaps off a box.

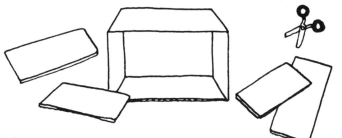

Cut the top off and then remove the flaps.

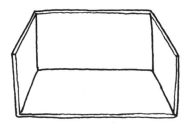

Cut your box on an angle.

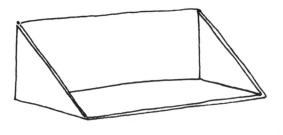

Remove the lid from a box.

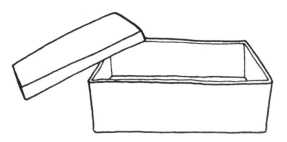

Collect boxes that are the same size and glue them together to make an apartment building.

Cut two tissue boxes in half. Glue the halves together to make a house.

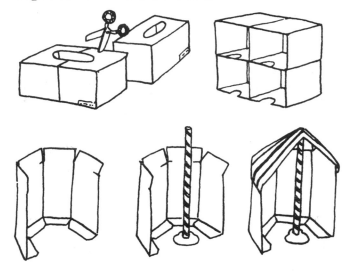

Open a box bottom. Cut down one side of the box and open it. Stand the box so the bottom flaps fold in and overlap. Cover the top with fabric and put a post in the middle to make a circus big top.

To cover your box:

You can paint it.

You can use self-adhesive contact paper.

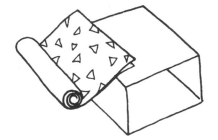

Use your imagination! Cover sections with Popsicle sticks, marbles, buttons, fabric, wood shavings, sequins or peanut shells!

You can cover the walls with paper. When you are lining the inside walls with paper, make careful measurements with a ruler.

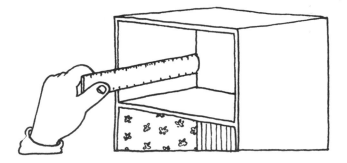

You can create windows. Tape a piece of plastic wrap to the back of the cut-out window. Make small fabric curtains.

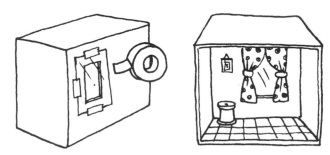

To make your diorama more interesting:

Look around your home or yard for interesting small objects.
You may find:

> A thimble
> Small boxes
> Paper clips
> Old jewellery
> Artificial flowers
> Small plastic toys

Be sure to ask permission before you take anything!

To create action in your diorama:

Draw, colour and cut out a figure with a tab at the bottom. Fold the tab and glue it to a strip. Cut a slot in the wall of your diorama and push the free end of the strip through the slot. Control the figure from the outside wall of your box.

Brass fasteners can make something turn on your wall.

Move an object by pulling on a looped string. To do this, pierce two holes in the wall of your box. Insert a long piece of string through the holes and tie the ends together at the back of the box. Tape a figure to the string. You can make the figure move by pulling the string at the back of the box.

TAB

Flowers

A. If you want to make flowers for a diorama, fringe a piece of paper and roll it into a tight cylinder. Tape the bottom and spread the fringes. To make a stem, poke a wire up the centre and tape in place.

B. You can also make a flower by stacking five or six pieces of tissue paper. Accordion fold the pieces together and wrap a wire or pipe cleaner around the middle. Pull up the layers of tissue paper to make the flower.

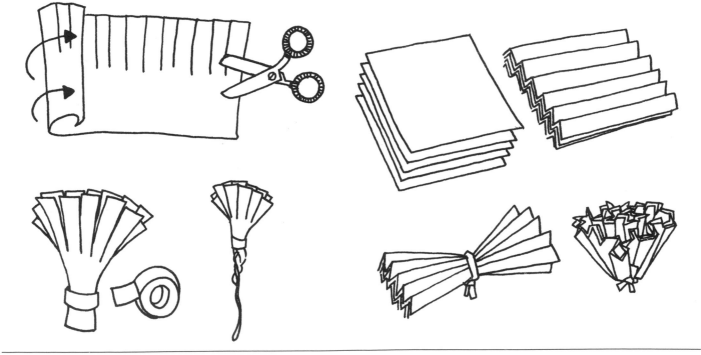

Use your dioramas for:

School projects: You can create a diorama to go with a story, research or a science project.

A centrepiece: Put it in the middle of your table or on a shelf.

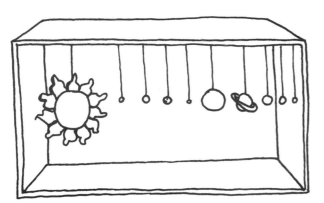

Part Three **Fun and Games**

This chapter has lots of fun outside activities that you can do with a group. You and your friends can get together and run a penny carnival, set up a mini-golf course, build forts with message systems or build an obstacle course. On a rainy day, you can make a camera that really works!

- For this chapter, you will need *lots* of boxes. Each time you have an empty cereal or tissue box, save it.

- When painting large boxes for the forts or the penny carnival, put newspaper under the boxes to catch paint drips and spills.

- When cutting heavy boxes, be sure to get an adult to help you.

- If you are holding an event such as a penny carnival or golf tournament, you may want to advertise. Make colourful posters and telephone your friends.

Mini-Golf

You can make your own mini-golf course with boxes, cardboard tubes, scissors and tape. Use your imagination and create some of your own ideas!

Make Your Own Golf Club

If you do not have a golf club, here is an easy one to make.

1 Cut four lines 5 cm (2 in.) long at one end of the tube.

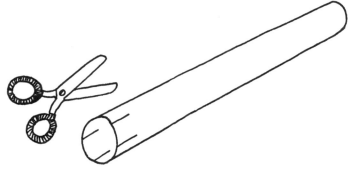

3 Close the box and secure it with tape. Now you have a golf club for hitting a ball. For a ball, you could use a golf ball, a tennis ball or a small rubber ball.

Materials

a small rectangular box
a long cardboard tube
Also: scissors, masking tape

2 In a large side of the box, cut a hole big enough for the tube to fit through and push the cut end of the tube through it. Inside the box, bend back the cut sections of the tube to create flaps. Tape the flaps to the inside of the box.

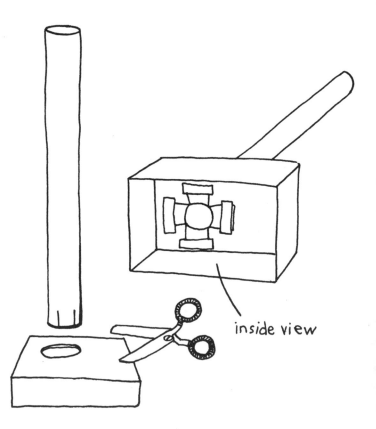

inside view

Try these golf activities

Up the Ramp

Materials

two boxes
Also: scissors,
 masking tape

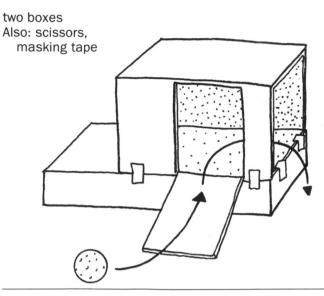

In and Out

Materials

two boxes
Also: scissors, masking tape

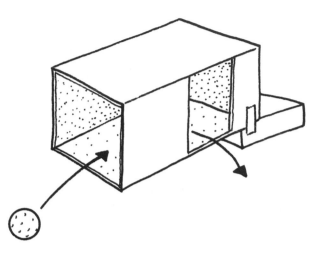

The Twister

Materials

a box
a long strip of cardboard or bristol board
Also: scissors, masking tape

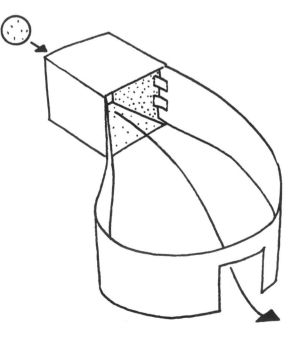

Through the House

Materials

a shoe box with a lid
Also: scissors, masking tape

cut and fold lid

cut a large hole in the back of the box

tape

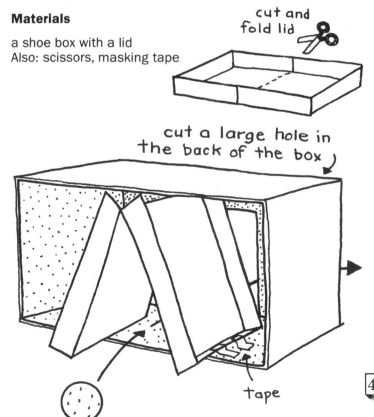

The Ballworks

Materials

five boxes
cardboard
Also: scissors, masking tape

hit ball here

The Swinging Tube

Materials

a box
a tube
string
a cardboard strip
Also: scissors, masking tape

push the tube to make it swing

Teeter-Totter

Materials

two identical rectangular boxes
Also: scissors, masking tape

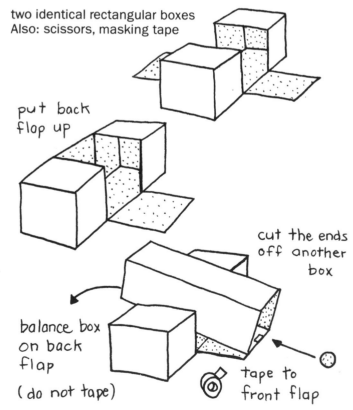

cut through middle of one box

put back flop up

cut the ends off another box

balance box on back flap

(do not tape)

tape to front flap

The Maze

Materials

five boxes
Also: scissors, masking tape

The boxes are open at the top

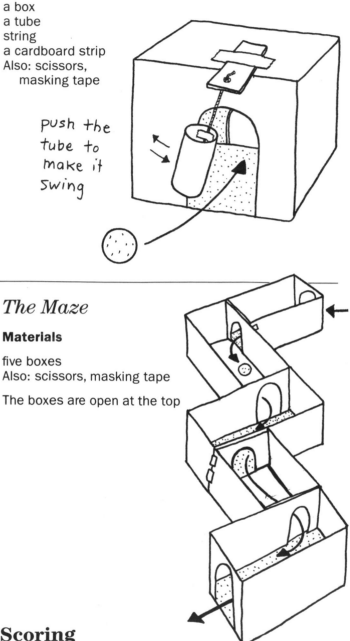

Scoring

If you wish, you can score your game. With a pencil and paper, keep track of the number of strokes it takes for a player to get through the game. The player with the lowest number of strokes wins the game.

Make Your Own Penny Carnival

Do you need to raise money for a good cause? Have a penny carnival! You can make tickets for each activity and sell them. What about prizes? You can buy snacks and small toys for prizes. Hold the event in a large yard — and make sure that you clean up afterwards.

Tell Your Fortune

Materials: a very large cardboard box, a blanket, a table, chairs, a ball, aluminum foil

Open up the box and drape a blanket over the top. Set up a table, chairs and a crystal ball. (To make a crystal ball, you can cover a ball with aluminum foil.) Dress up in a fortune-teller's costume.

Go Fishing

Materials: a large box, a stick, string, a paper clip, coloured paper and decorations, prizes

Decorate the box like a fish pond. Make a fishing pole with a long stick, a string and a hook made from a paper clip.

Cut out and decorate paper fish and write a number on each one. Have someone sit at the bottom of the box and clip a "fish" to the hook. Each number represents a different prize.

White Elephant Sale

Make a table out of a large box. Bring in your old toys and books and sell them.

Bicycle Challenge

Make an obstacle course with boxes. If a person can weave in and out of the boxes on a bicycle without falling, he or she receives a prize.

Popcorn and Lemonade Stand

Take a large box and make a stand. Everyone gets hungry or thirsty at a carnival.

Ring Toss

Materials: a large box, 8 cardboard tubes, scissors, masking tape, markers, large heavy-weight paper plates, prizes

Open up the box. Cut 4 lines 5 cm (2 in.) long at the bottom of each tube and fold back the cut sections to create flaps. Tape the flaps to the box. Write a different number under each tube. Make rings by taking large paper plates and cutting out the middle areas. Throw a ring onto a tube to win a prize.

Feed the Monster

Materials: a large box, paint, scissors, beanbags, prizes

Open up a large box. Draw a large monster face with a giant mouth and cut out the mouth. Each person pays for three beanbag throws. If a bean bag lands in the mouth, the thrower receives a prize.

Make a Cartridge Pinhole Camera

In making this camera, you make a *box* that fits into a cartridge of film. A cartridge pinhole camera is easy to use because you can load and unload the camera in daylight and take at least 12 pictures without changing the cartridge. Have your photo dealer process the film. When making this camera, be very exact with your measurements!

Materials

a 126-size cartridge of KODAK GOLD 200 Film for colour prints
a piece of thin black cardboard, 3.2 cm x 14.6 cm (1¼ in. x 5¾ in.)
black tape (or masking tape coloured black)
a No. 10 (medium-sized) sewing needle
a square of heavy aluminum foil, 2.5 cm x 2.5 cm (1 in. x 1 in.)
a piece of rigid black cardboard, 3.8 cm x 7 cm (1½ in. x 2¾ in.)
a square of black paper, 2.5 cm x 2.5 cm (1 in. x 1 in.)
2 strong rubber bands (that will hold the box to the cartridge firmly in place)
a nickel (or medium-sized coin)
Also: Olfa touch knife, pencil, ruler

Assembling the Camera

1 Measure and mark the large piece of black cardboard into 4 sections, each 3.6 cm (1⁷⁄₁₆ in.) wide.

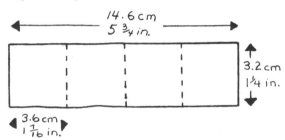

2 Score the cardboard along the lines you've just drawn. This will make it easier to fold the cardboard.

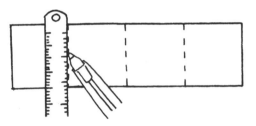

3 Fold the cardboard into a box and tape the edges together with the black tape. This is your camera box.

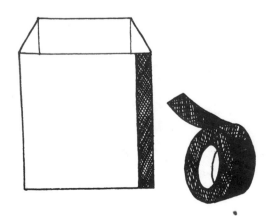

4 Using only *the point* of the sewing needle, make a *very tiny* pinhole in the centre of the aluminum foil. When you make the hole, put the foil on a hard flat surface.

5 Cut a square hole 1.3 cm x 1.3 cm (½ in. x ½ in.) in the centre of the rigid black cardboard.

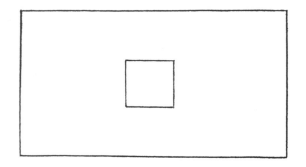

6 Centre the pinhole in the foil over the square opening in the small piece of cardboard. Tape the foil to the cardboard on all four edges.

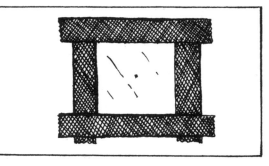

7 To make the shutter, put the small piece of black paper over the pinhole and tape it along the top edge. Use a small piece of masking tape at the bottom of the black paper to hold it down between exposures (pictures).

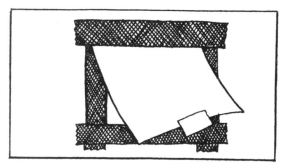

8 Using black tape, tape the cardboard with the pinhole to the box, shutter side out. Use plenty of tape and make sure all the edges are taped together so that no light can get into the camera box.

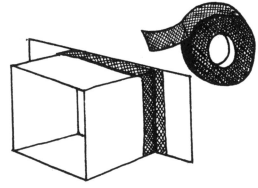

9 Put the camera box that you have made into the square opening of the film cartridge. This should be a tight fit so that no light can get into the camera.

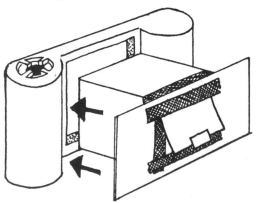

10 Use the two strong rubber bands to hold the camera in place.

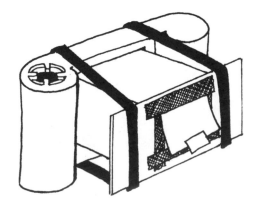

11 Insert the edge of a nickel in the round opening on the top of the film cartridge.

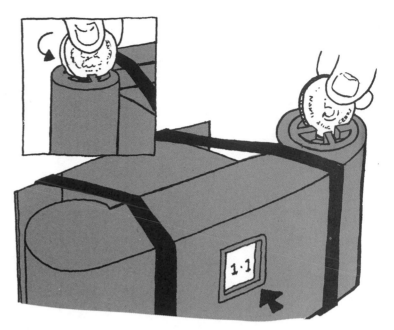

12 To advance the film in the cartridge, turn the coin counter-clockwise. The yellow paper (visible in the small window on the label side of the film cartridge) should move. The film has borders and numbers printed on it. Turn the coin slowly until the third and fourth numbers in each series on the yellow paper show in the window. The film will then be in the proper position for picture taking. For the second picture, turn to the third and fourth number 2.

13 To take pictures: Your camera must be *very still* while you are taking a picture. Tape your camera to a table, window sill, chair, rock or other rigid surface. Aim your camera by looking over the top surface.

14 Lift the small piece of tape at the bottom of the black piece of paper. Hold it up for a few seconds. Make sure you don't jiggle the camera when you lift the paper. Use the tape on the black paper to hold the paper over the pinhole after each exposure (picture). This prevents light from entering your camera and spoiling your photos. Advance your film before taking your next picture. Take pictures in lots of light. Take three pictures of each scene, each time holding up the black piece of paper (to expose the film) for a different length of time. See the table below.

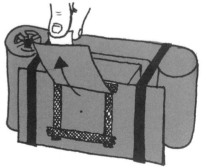

Adapted courtesy of Eastman Kodak Company.

Exposure Time
Here are exposure recommendations for your pinhole camera. These recommendations are *approximate*. It's a good idea to make three different exposures for each scene to be sure you'll get a good picture.

Film	Bright Sun	Cloudy Bright
KODAK GOLD 200	1½ sec	4 sec
	3 sec	7 sec
	6 sec	12–15 sec

Make Two Clubhouses with a Box Message System

Materials

2 large boxes
a small box, such as a tissue box
tempera or other paint and paint brush
a long piece of string (kite string, if available)
   The length of the string should be double
   the distance between the clubhouses.
a small paper clip
Also: scissors, utility knife, masking tape

1 Have an adult cut a door in each of the large boxes to make your clubhouse.

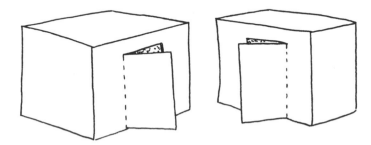

2 Cut a window on the top side area of each box. The windows of the two boxes should face each other.

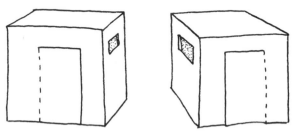

3 Make two small holes under each window. The holes are for your message system.

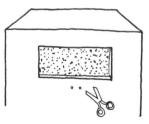

4 Paint and decorate the two box clubhouses. Add signs, flags or banners.

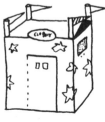

5 To make the box message system, tape all ends of the small box closed. Cut a small flap door on the top side of the box and put a piece of tape on the flap door to secure it to the box.

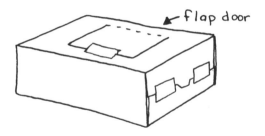

← flap door

6 Make two parallel holes on each end of the box. Make the holes big enough that a paper clip can slide through them.

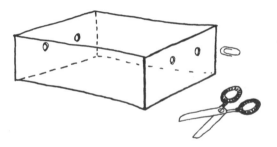

7 To attach the message system to the clubhouses, tie one end of the string to the paper clip. Push the paper clip through the holes in the message box and clubhouses as shown.

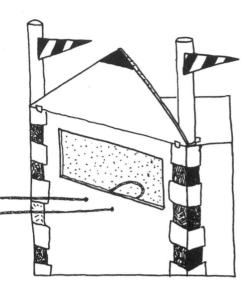

Start here

8 Tie the piece of string with the paper clip to the other loose end of string. Make a secure knot and cut off the paper clip.

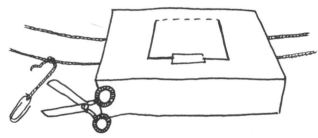

9 Slide the knot inside the message box and tape it to the bottom.

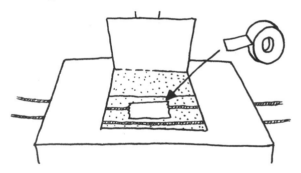

10 Place your message inside the box. Close the flap again, using the piece of tape. If you wish, leave a pencil and paper in your box.

11 Now you are ready to send the message. One person inside the other clubhouse pulls on *one side* of the string, hand over hand. As the string is pulled, the box will move along to the other clubhouse. To receive the message, a person reaches out the window of the clubhouse and opens the flap of the small box.

Wiggle and Jump Your Way Through an Obstacle Course

If you have a lot of boxes, it's fun to make an obstacle course. How quickly can you go from start to finish? Time each other using a watch.

With the box obstacle course, make sure that the holes in the boxes are big enough. You don't want anyone to get stuck!

Wiggle Through

Wiggle through a long box.

Jumping Boxes

Join three medium-sized boxes by poking small holes in them and fastening twist-ties or pipe cleaners through the holes. Jump into each box.

Don't Spill

Carry a small open box of popcorn on your head without spilling it.

Crawl Through

Cut two large round holes in a box and crawl through.

Walk-a-box

Cut a hole in the bottom of a medium-sized box. Slide the box up to your knees and walk without holding the box with your hands.

The Maze

Use chairs, blankets and a box to create a crawl-through maze.

The Slide

If you have a little hill, open up a large box and make a slide.

Hopping Box

Squash your two feet into a small box such as a shoe box, and hop from a start line to a finish line.

The Finish

Make a finish line by attaching a string and banners between two boxes.

Part Four Boxes You Can Wear

A tin man, a triceratops, an airplane, a lion — you can make all sorts of costumes with boxes. You'll have fun surprising your friends with your amazing box costumes.

Tips

- If your head is covered with your box costume, *do not* go outside. It is not safe to wear large head coverings when trick or treating. It is safer to wear these costumes indoors.

- Be sure you can breathe easily when you are wearing your mask. If not, remove it immediately.

- If you are using a utility knife to cut heavy boxes, ask an adult to do the cutting for you.

- You can reinforce moving parts with twist-ties.

- Make *large* eye-holes or eye areas in masks so you can see easily.

- You can recycle many costumes by using them again for other purposes. Masks make interesting wall-hangings or room decorations. Costumes made from large boxes can be used again for storage or toy boxes later.

- Make large enough body holes in your boxes so that you can move comfortably.

Make an Airplane

Materials

a large box big enough to cover half your
   body
tempera or other paint and a paint brush
aluminum foil (optional)
a large brass fastener or large paper clip
a large sheet of bristol board
scrap paper and stickers (optional)
Also: scissors, utility knife, masking
   tape, glue, stapler, twist-ties (optional)

1 Cut the flaps off your box. Stand the box so that the closed bottom is now the top.

2 Draw wings on two sides of your box. Each wing should be a little longer than your arm and about 30 cm (12 in.) wide. Make sure the wings are directly across from one another.

3 On the top of the box, draw a rectangle big enough for your head to fit through. The rectangle must *not* reach as far as the edges of the box.

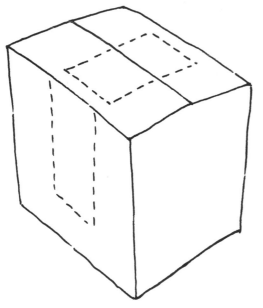

4 Ask an adult to help you cut around the sides and the bottom of the wings. *Do not cut the top of the wings.* Cut out the rectangular head-hole.

5 Paint your wings one colour and the body another colour.

6 To make a propeller, cut two strips of bristol board and shape the ends into points. Cover them with aluminum foil if you wish. Pierce a small hole in the middle of each propeller blade and fasten them onto the front of the airplane with a large brass fastener.

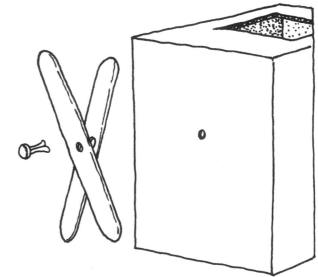

Optional: To strengthen the wing areas, use sharp scissors to punch four pairs of holes above the wings as shown. Insert a twist-tie into each pair of holes and twist it inside the box.

7 To make a base for your windshield, cut a piece of bristol board the same width as your box and about 25 cm (10 in.) long. Make three folds in the board, each 7.5 cm (3 in.) apart, and fold it into the shape of a triangular prism (the narrow strip is your tab). Fasten the prism closed with tape. This is the base for your windshield. From the bristol board, cut a square windshield frame the same width as your base and staple it to the base. (Put plastic wrap in the frame for a window, if you like.) Attach the windshield to the plane with twist-ties, as shown, and glue.

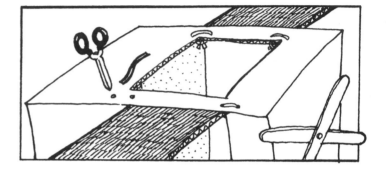

twist-tie

8 To make a tail, cut a piece of bristol board 35 cm x 35 cm (14 in. x 14 in.) and fold it into quarters. Open it and cut from the bottom middle point to the centre. Fold the bristol board in half lengthwise and put glue between the top halves. Fold the bottom halves out. Cut the top area so that it resembles a tail wing. Attach the tail to the back top area of the box using masking tape.

9 Paint or glue on numbers and decals, or add a dashboard and a steering wheel. You can also cut flaps into the wings. Dress the part by wearing goggles and a scarf!

Variation

Make a big bird by covering the box with paper feathers. Cut out a paper mask and add a beak, eyeholes, paper feathers and string ties.

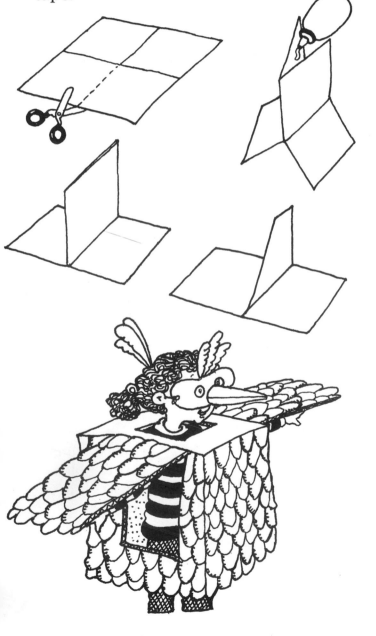

Make Your Own Triceratops

Materials

a small heavy cardboard box with flaps that can fit over your head
a package of small origami paper or small squares of coloured paper
tempera or other paint and paint brush
3 pieces of construction paper
2 small identical plastic bottles or 2 identical lids from shampoo bottles
2 sheets of bristol board
scraps of paper and foil
string
Also: utility knife, masking tape, stapler

1 Cut the flap off one side of the box and save it. Cut two-thirds of the way down the corners of that side and fold down this piece.

2 Cut two half circles on the sides of the box as shown.

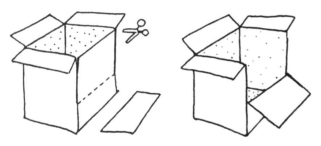

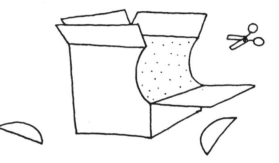

3 Put the box over your head as shown. Ask a friend to mark the position of your eyes. Take the box off your head and have an adult cut a strip across the box where the eye marks are. Cut "V" shapes on each end of the strip. This will be your dinosaur's mouth and your eye-slot.

4 Cut in half the end flap you saved. Staple these half pieces between the side flaps and top flap as shown.

5 Cut two small round holes at the top of the box for eyes.

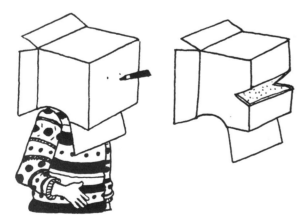

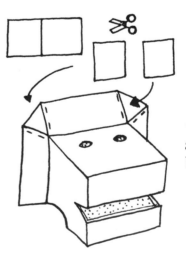

6 Paint the head one colour and the flaps behind the head another colour. Staple squares of paper around the flaps as shown.

7 To make each horn (you'll need three), roll a piece of construction paper into a cone, tape it and trim the end straight across. Cut four small flaps and fold the flaps back. Staple or tape the horns on by the flaps.

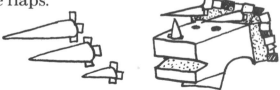

8 Push the bottles or lids into the eye-holes and tape. Make paper teeth and glue them in the mouth. Cut out and glue on two round pieces of paper for nostrils.

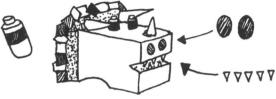

9 To make a scaly body, round the corners on two pieces of bristol board. Cover one piece with overlapping pieces of origami paper or small scales cut from coloured paper.

10 To wear the body, punch holes in the shoulders and waist and tie string between the holes, as shown.

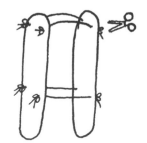

11 *More ideas:* For a tail, roll a large cone and attach it to the back piece of bristol board. For claws, cut out paper claw shapes and attach them to gloves.

12 Try on your costume. Tuck the front flap of your mask under the front body piece. When you walk with your costume on, remember that a triceratops weighed about 12 tonnes!

Variation

Make a lion by painting the face yellow and the back flaps orange. Attach whiskers, large teeth, a nose and ears. Draw a furry chest on the body piece. Attach a nylon stocking tail.

63

Make a Sports Car

Materials
a large box
2 boxes from rolls of plastic wrap or foil
3 sheets of bristol board or heavy paper
plastic wrap
aluminum foil
a round lid from a large plastic container
a toilet-paper tube
a belt or long piece of cord
yellow paper
2 foil tart tins
Also: scissors, utility knife, masking tape, glue or stapler, markers

1 With an adult's help, cut the flaps off your box and cut a large hole in the middle of the bottom. The hole should be large enough for you to step into the box and pull it up to your waist.

2 To make the front of the car, curve a piece of bristol board around one end of your box. Fold the top of the bristol board over the edge of the box and secure it with masking tape. Secure the bottom with tape. You can make different models by making folds across the bristol board.

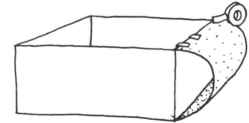

3 To make the back end of the car, cut one-third of the way down the back corner seams of your box. Fold the side corners down to make triangular flaps and secure the back corners of the box to the flaps with tape or staples. Cover the back end with a piece of bristol board. Tape it as shown, leaving the sides untaped. You can curve the top back to make fins.

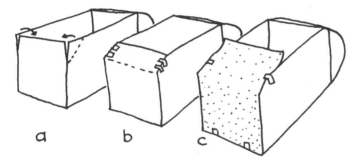

a   b   c

4 To make the sides of the car, lay one side of your box on bristol board or heavy paper. Trace around the shape and add tabs. Repeat on another sheet with the other side. Cut out the two shapes. Place the sides on your box and tape the tabs to it. Tuck the back tabs into the sides you left open in step 3 and tape securely.

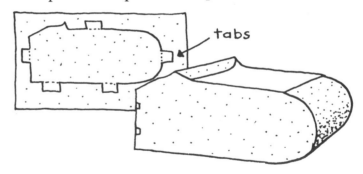

tabs

5 Make the windshield by cutting a curved piece of bristol board as shown. It should be wider than the width of your car. Cut out the middle area and lay a piece of plastic wrap over the hole. Staple or glue the wrap in place and cut off any extra.

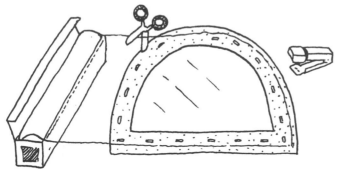

6 To attach the windshield to the car, curve the windshield around the top of the box and secure the bottom edges with masking tape. Make bristol board struts to strengthen the windshield.

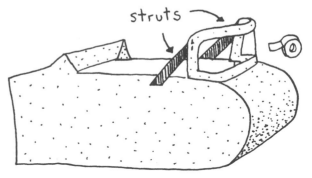

struts

7 To make bumpers, cover the two long rectangular boxes with foil. Attach one to the front and one to the back of the car with masking tape. Make headlights by gluing yellow circles of paper into the tart tins and securing them to the bumper.

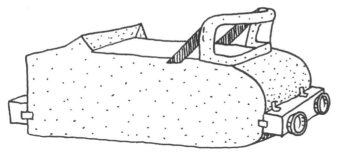

9 To make a safety-belt strap, attach an old belt or cord.

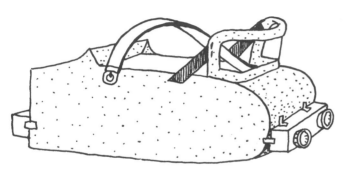

8 Use a small box or a piece of bristol board to make a dash board. To make the steering wheel, make four short cuts at each end of the toilet-paper tube. Bend the edges back at one end and tape that end to the round plastic lid. To attach the steering wheel to the car, cut a hole, the same diameter as the tube, in the dash board. Insert the tube and fold back the flaps. Tape them in place or leave your steering wheel free to turn. Draw on a speedometer, fuel gauge and radio.

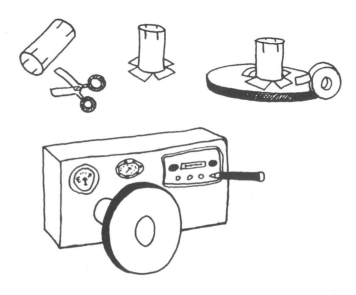

10 Other things you can add:

fins

windshield wipers

mirror

doors

licence plate

Wheels

Dress for driving. Wear sunglasses for sunny days.

Variations

1 *Make a snowmobile*

Add skis and a track.

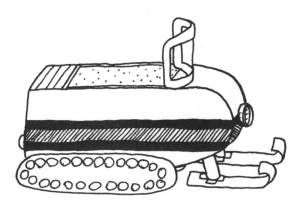

2 *Make an old-fashioned car*

Add large fins, large bumpers and a hood ornament.

Make a Tin Man

You may find it a little difficult to see out of this costume. Be sure to only wear it indoors.

Materials

a box large enough to fit over your chest
2 sheets of bristol board
aluminum foil
2 toilet-paper tubes
2 tissue boxes (optional)
Also: scissors, utility knife, clear tape, masking tape

1 To make the head, cut out a piece of bristol board 25 cm x 78 cm (10 in. x 31 in.). Cover one side of the bristol board with aluminum foil. Wrap the extra foil over the edges and secure it with tape.

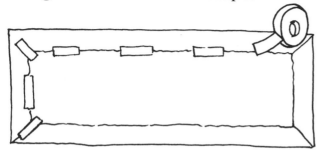

2 Wrap the bristol board loosely around your head and ask a friend to mark where your eyes are. Remove the bristol board and cut cross shapes at these points. Fold back the cut areas and tape them inside the mask.

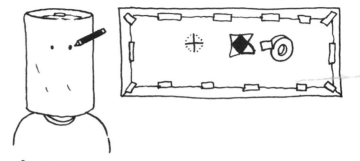

3 Mark the nose and cut a cross shape 5 cm x 5 cm (2 in. x 2 in.). Fold back the cut areas inside the mask. Cover a tube with aluminum foil (leave both ends open) then push the tube through the nose area. Tape the nose flaps to the tube. Make four small cuts at the end of the tube inside the mask to make flaps. Fold the flaps back and tape them to the bristol board.

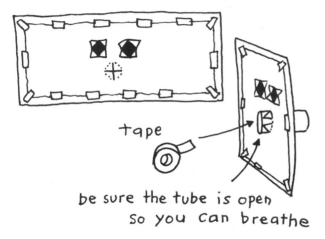

tape

be sure the tube is open so you can breathe

4 Roll a piece of aluminum foil into a mouth. Shape and tape it to your mask.

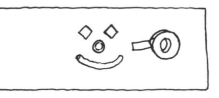

5 Loosely wrap the bristol board around your head and secure it with tape.

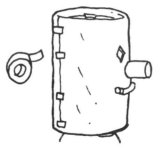

6 To make an oil-can hat, cut a piece of aluminum foil big enough to wrap around your mask. Tape the bottom of the foil inside the top edge of the mask. Wrap the second tube in foil, hold it just above the middle of your mask and pull the top edge of the foil around it. Secure with tape.

leave the end of the tube open

7 To make the body, have an adult cut a hole in the bottom of the box big enough for your head to fit through. Cut the flaps off the box.

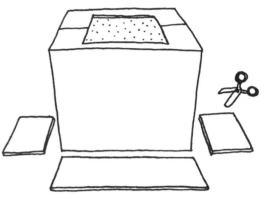

8 Cut arm notches on both sides of the box, as shown.

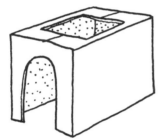

9 Cover the box with aluminum foil and tape in place.

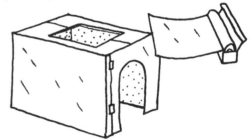

10 To make arm and leg bands, cut pieces of bristol board large enough to wrap around your arms and legs. Cover one side of each piece with foil and shape them into cylinders. Tape securely. Draw studs on the head, body, arm and leg pieces.

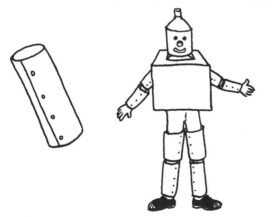

11 You can make shoes by covering tissue boxes with foil. Use heavy cardboard to make an axe to go with your costume.

Variation

Make a robot by using a box for a head. Glue paper dials and real buttons on the box that covers your body.

Make a Moon Suit

Materials

a box big enough to fit over your head
a large cereal box
2 small boxes, one smaller than the other
aluminum foil
an elastic band (or hair elastic)
a toilet-paper tube
2 brass fasteners
2 long strips of bristol board (or ribbon)
scraps of paper and stickers
Also: scissors, utility knife, masking tape,
    compass (or tool for making holes),
    twist-ties

1 To make your helmet, cut the flaps off the first box, place the box over your head and mark the position of your nose. Have an adult cut a hole around this mark.

2 Cut round notches at the bottom sides of the box, so that the box will sit on your shoulders.

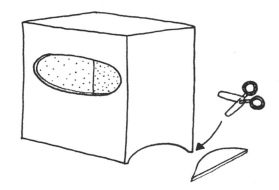

3 Cover the box with aluminum foil. To fit the foil around the face hole, pierce a hole in the foil in the middle of the face area. Carefully cut it as shown and fold the edges back. Decorate your helmet with coloured paper or stickers.

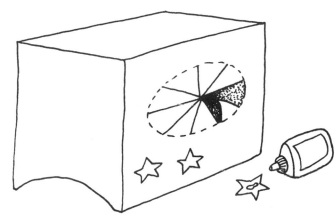

4 To make a space back-pack, tape the top of the cereal box closed. About one-third of the way down the box, cut around the front and sides (but *not* the back) of the box.

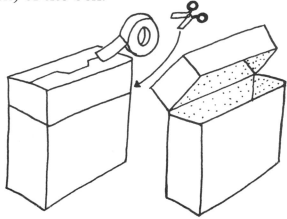

5 Cover the box with aluminum foil. It is easiest to wrap the bottom of the box first, tucking the extra foil inside the box. Then wrap the top of the box separately. Decorate your space pack with strips of coloured paper. You can also add side boxes covered with foil.

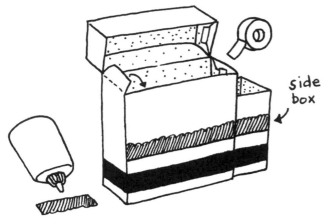

side box

6 To make a latch so that you can open and close your space pack, wrap an elastic band around a brass fastener. Insert the fastener into the top middle area of the box, as shown. Stretch the elastic to see how far down it will reach and mark that with a dot. Insert a brass fastener at the dot so that the elastic will fit around it and hold the box closed.

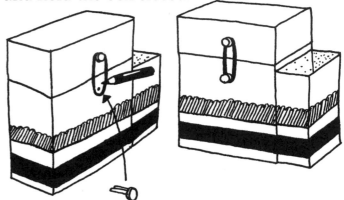

7 To make a space camera, cut a round hole in your smallest box big enough to fit the toilet-paper tube.

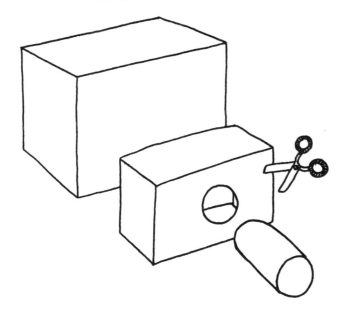

8 Wrap the two boxes with aluminum foil. Pierce the foil over the hole and tuck in any extra. Wrap the tube with coloured paper or foil.

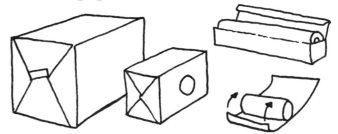

9 Insert the tube into the hole. Attach the smaller box to the other box.

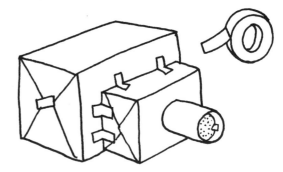

10 To make straps for the camera and space pack, pierce two holes at the ends of each of the strips of bristol board or ribbon. Pierce two holes in each of the back top corners of the space pack. (This is easily done by opening up the lid and using scissors or a compass. Have an adult help you.) Loop a twist-tie through each set of the holes.

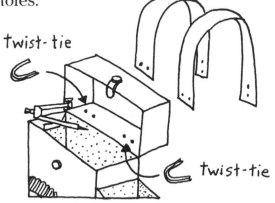

twist-tie

twist-tie

11 Pierce the top edges of the back of the camera as in step 10. Insert twist-ties in each set of holes.

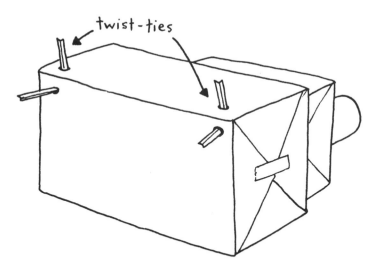

twist-ties

12 Insert the twist-ties of the space pack into the holes of the strap. Twist the ties and secure them to the space pack with masking tape. Attach the camera to the straps in the same way.

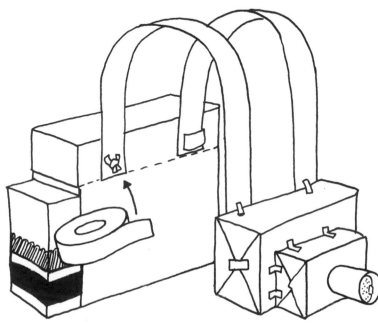

13 Now put on your outfit! It looks best if you wear white under it.

Part Five Let's Put On a Show

Do you like putting on a puppet show or taking part in a play? There are lots of ideas in this chapter for different kinds of puppet theatres, puppets, masks, musical instruments and props.

Tips

- Try writing your own plays or drama productions. You can base your story on a favourite book, short story or comic book. Or you can use your imagination and come up with a new story.

- Start saving empty boxes. Store small boxes in a garbage bag or large box. Save cardboard tubes from toilet paper and gift wrap. After a birthday party, keep the left-over wrapping paper.

- Practise with your puppets until they develop a personality. Through using various voices and hand movements, you can create different characters. Extra details such as earrings, hair styles, hats and bow ties add to the puppets' personalities.

- You can use the ideas from Part Four to make costumes to wear on stage.

- A musical band is more fun with a group of friends. Try putting on a group performance.

- It is fun to have someone videotape your performance.

Make a Popping Monster Puppet

Materials

a small rectangular box such as a tissue box
construction paper or gift wrap
a discarded sock
yarn
a needle and thread
an elastic band (or hair elastic)
buttons
6 brass fasteners
a wood dowel or a straight wooden stick
shoelace or heavy string
ribbon, lace, felt, pipe cleaners, etc.
Also: scissors, clear tape, twist-ties, glue

1 To prepare the container the puppet will pop out of, open one end of the box and cut the flaps off that end.

2 Cut a round hole in the other end of the box. The hole should be at least 7.5 cm (3 in.) in diameter.

3 Cover the box with paper and secure it with tape. Tuck the paper over the edges of the open end of the box and the hole, securing them with tape. Decorate your box.

4 To make the monster puppet, cut off the sock above the ankle. Save the top part of the sock.

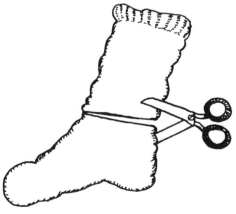

5 To make the head, stuff the toe of the sock with yarn. Wrap a twist-tie or elastic band around the sock below the stuffed toe. Make the head small enough that it can go through the hole in the box.

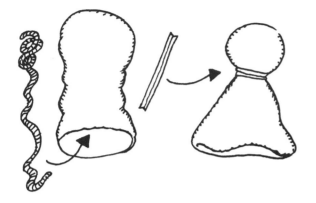

6 Sew on buttons for the eyes, nose and mouth. You can use felt and glue instead of buttons. Add wild-looking hair, large ears, teeth and spots.

7 To attach the puppet to the box, poke six holes around the hole you cut in the box. Stretch the bottom of the sock over the large hole. Push the brass fasteners through the sock and then through the small holes. Open the fasteners inside the box.

8 Push the wooden dowel or stick through the bottom of the box and up into the puppet's head. Wrap a twist-tie or a ribbon around the sock puppet's middle to create a long neck.

9 To create arms, take two pieces of shoelace or heavy string about 7.5 cm (3 in.) long. Cut hands from the piece of sock that you have saved and sew them onto the shoelaces. Sew the arms onto the puppet below the neck. When you twist the stick quickly, the arms will fly around.

10 Pull the monster into the box by pulling down the stick. Then make the monster pop up by pushing the stick up.

Variations

Make a puppet that fits on your hand. Instead of using a stick, pull your arm up and down through the box.

Make a puppet and a box home for your puppet. Pull your puppet in and out of the box house.

Wiggle a Pig's Nose

Materials

a rectangular box (such as a tissue box)
pink tissue paper or other paper
an egg carton
a toilet-paper tube
scraps of coloured paper
Also: scissors, clear tape, masking tape,
glue, twist-tie

1 Cut one end off the box. To do this easily, open up the glued flaps and cut them from the box. Save them for later.

2 Wrap the box with pink tissue paper or other paper and tape it in place.

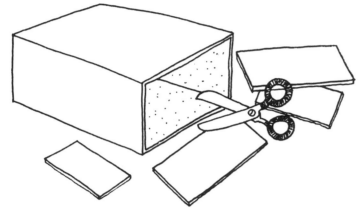

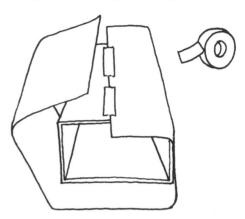

3 To cover the closed end of the box, fold the paper as if you were wrapping a present. Secure the folded paper with tape.

4 At the open end of the box, slit the four corners of paper as far as the box. Fold the four flaps of paper inside the box and secure them with tape.

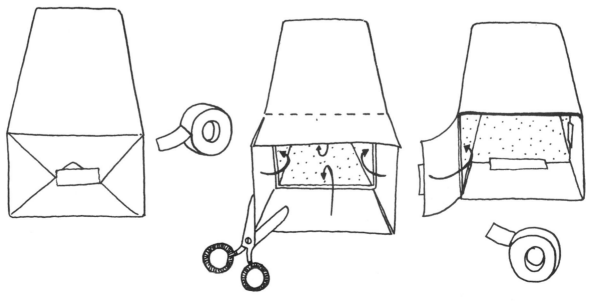

5 To make the pig's eyes, cut the egg carton in half. Cut off the end two segments and trim the edges. Cut out two round yellow pieces of paper for eyeballs and glue them into the bottom of each cup. Small pupils can be added using round pieces of green paper.

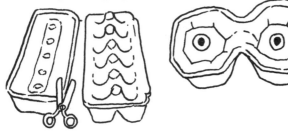

6 To make the snout, wrap a toilet-paper tube with pink tissue paper or other paper and tape it in place. Cover one end of the tube with tissue paper and leave the other end open. Carefully draw two nostrils on the covered end of the tube.

7 To make the ears, draw pig's ears on the flaps you saved from step 1 and cut them out, making a tab at the bottom of each ear. Slit each tab up the middle. Cover the pig's ears and tabs with pink paper and secure the paper with tape.

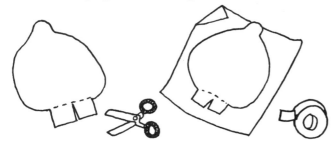

8 To make the tail, cover a twist-tie with pink paper. Secure the paper with tape and roll the covered twist-tie into a spiral shape.

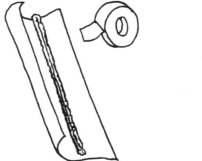

9 Place the eyes towards the closed end of the box. Below the eyes mark a dot. Draw a hole the size of the open end of the tube around the dot and cut out the hole.

10 Cut four short slits at the open end of the tube and push that end through the hole. Fold the cut sections back and secure them to the inside of the box with tape.

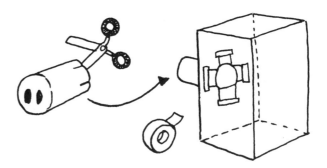

11 Using white glue, attach the eyes immediately above the snout. Draw a mouth below.

12 Bend the ears, so they curve forward. Place one ear on a top corner of the box. Tape the top half of the tab to the top of the box and tape the bottom half of the tab to the side of the box. Repeat this with the other ear.

13 Tape the tail to the back of the puppet. If you wish, give your pig a shirt collar and tie or a fancy hat. Put your index finger through the tube from inside the box to make the snout move up and down!

Variation

Make an Owl Puppet

1 You can make an owl by adding a beak, wings, eyes and feathers to an empty tissue box.

cut a small hole here

2 Tape a looped twist-tie to the bottom of the beak. Put your finger through the loop and make the beak move up and down.

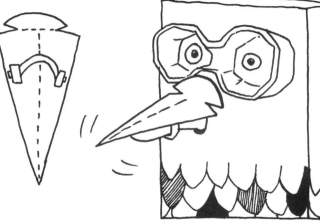

Make an Elephant Mask

You may find it a little difficult to see out of this mask. Be sure to only use it for indoor performances.

Materials

a shoebox that can fit over your head
stiff wrapping paper and construction paper
2 identical small lids
scraps of paper
Also: scissors, clear tape, stapler

1 About one-third of the way from one end, draw a vertical line. Do the same on the other side. Cut along these lines.

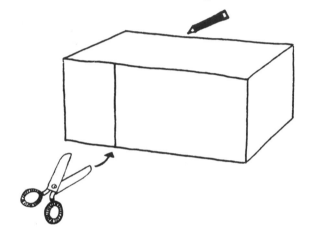

2 Place the box open side down. Bend the box so that the small part overlaps into the larger part. Secure with staples. Cover the staples inside the box with tape.

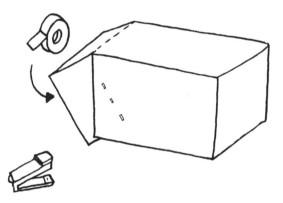

3 Cut up the centre of the box. Overlap the two halves into each other so that the box is tapered. Staple the overlapping sections at the end of the box.

4 Cut a mouth at that same end of the box. You may need adult help to do this. This will serve as your eye-hole.

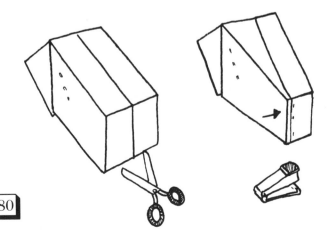

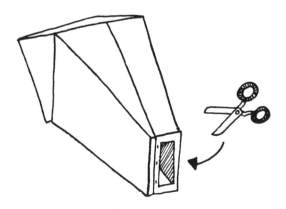

5 Cover the outside of the box with stiff wrapping paper or construction paper. Tuck any extra paper inside the box and secure it with tape. Cut paper away from the eye-hole.

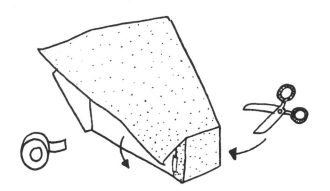

6 Using heavy paper, cut two large ears with tabs. Slit each tab and attach the ears as in step 12, page 79.

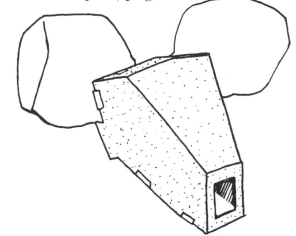

7 To make the trunk, cut out eight strips of paper. The strips should gradually get smaller, going from 10 cm x 4 cm (4 in. x 1½ in.) to 2 cm x 4 cm (¾ in. x 1½ in.). Shape each strip into a loop and secure it with tape. Loosely attach the loops together with tape, going from largest to smallest.

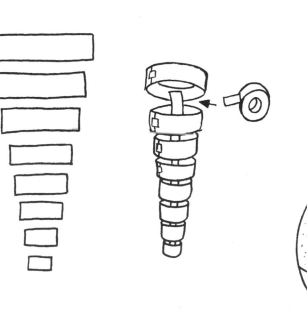

8 To attach the trunk to the head, cut a strip of paper 6 cm x 6 cm (2½ in. x 2½ in.). Tape it to the top edge of the front of the box. Tape the top of the trunk under the strip. Fold and tape the edges of the strip around the trunk.

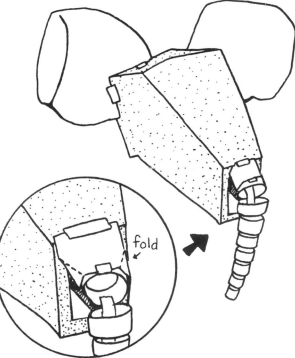

fold

9 Tape two small lids to the box for eyes. Add pupils.

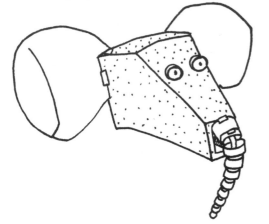

10 To make the tusks, roll two paper cones, tape them and trim the ends straight across. Make cuts halfway through each cone as shown so that you can curve the tusks.

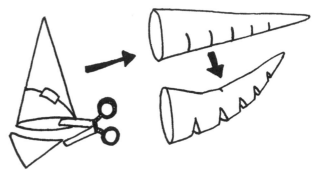

11 Cut flaps at the end of the tusks and tape the flaps onto the box on either side of the trunk.

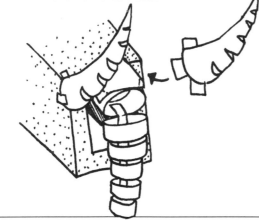

12 Put on your mask. You may need ties to keep it on firmly. To make these, punch holes in the back part of the box. Put a string through these holes and tie the ends under your chin.

Variations

By changing the ears and nose, you can make different animals.

Puppy dog   *Cow*

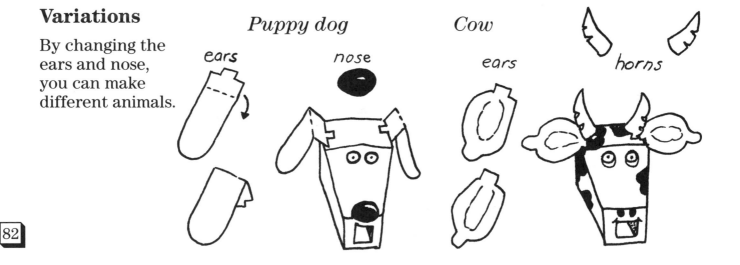

ears   nose   ears   horns

Make Your Own Musical Box Band

Materials

small to medium-sized boxes
aluminum foil or waxed paper
elastic bands
cardboard tubes
heavy paper
dry peas or beans
metal lids from jars and cooking pots
foil tart tin
a plastic tab from a bread bag
bobby pins
brass fasteners
⚠ Also: scissors, Olfa touch knife, masking
  tape, twist-tie

Box Kazoo

1 Remove the flaps from one end of a small box, such as a candy box.

2 Wrap aluminum foil or waxed paper over the open end and secure it with an elastic band.

3 Make a hole at the other end of the box. Place your mouth over the hole and sing or hum. You will hear a vibrating sound.

hole

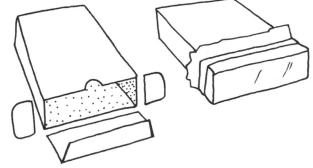

Shaker

1 Fill a small box with dry peas or beans.

2 Close the flaps and secure them with tape. Decorate your shaker.

Tube and Box Kazoo

1 Cover one end of an empty cardboard tube with aluminum foil or waxed paper, securing it with an elastic band. Pierce two holes in the tube near the open end.

holes

2 Close the open end of an empty small box and secure it with tape. Cut a round hole, the same diameter as the tube, in the side of the box.

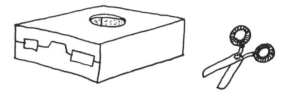

3 Push the covered end of the tube into the round hole of the box. Secure the tube to the box with tape. Decorate the box.

4 Hold the box and cover the open end of the tube with your mouth. Sing into the tube and it will vibrate. Try pressing the one or two holes in the tube while you sing.

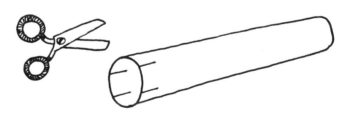

Cymbal

1 Close the flaps at the top of a medium-sized box and secure them with tape. Cut a small hole in the top of the box that is big enough for a cardboard tube to fit through.

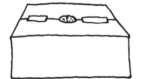

2 At one end of a long cardboard tube, cut four lines that are 5 cm (2 in.) long.

3 Fold back the areas between the cut lines to create flaps. Place the end of the tube with flaps under the middle of a metal lid and secure the flaps to the bottom of the lid with masking tape.

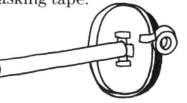

4 Insert the other end of the tube through the hole to the bottom of the box. Secure the tube to the box with tape. Use a spoon or a stick to play your cymbal.

Cymbal Set

Take a long low box and make three holes in the top area. Find three different-sized lids and secure them to tubes. Each lid will make a different sound, depending on its size. Insert the tubes into the holes and tape them to the box.

Box Guitar

1 Tape a foil tart tin, open side down, to the middle of a small box. If you do not have a tart tin, use a small lid or an empty spool.

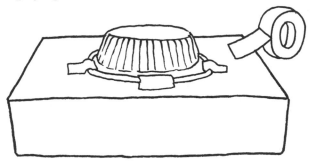

2 On each end of the box, make three small cuts with a knife.

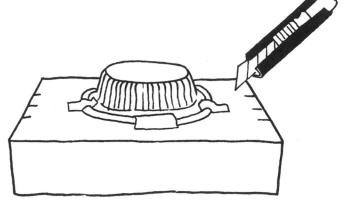

3 Stretch three elastic bands over the box and tart tin, fitting each band into a cut at each end of the box.

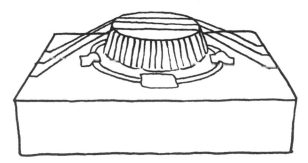

4 Wrap a twist-tie around the three elastics between the tin and the end of the box.

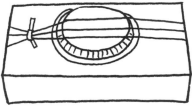

5 Strum the elastic bands of your guitar with a plastic bread bag tab.

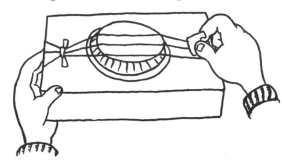

Strummer

1 Close a small box and secure it with tape.

2 Place a row of six bobby pins or brass fasteners along the edge of the box. Bend them open and tape them to the box. Bend some more open than others. Put some on other areas of the box if you wish.

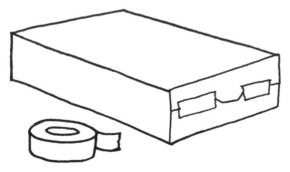

3 Pluck the ends of the bobby pins or brass fasteners using your thumb or index finger.

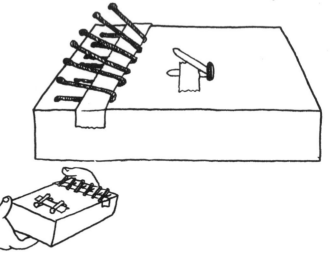

Clinker

1 Cut a tissue box around the middle on three sides. Bend the cut sections back.

2 On each of the sides now touching each other, tape a metal jar lid as shown. The lids should hit one another when your clinker is closed.

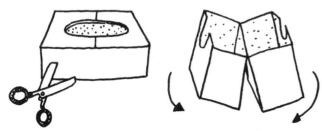

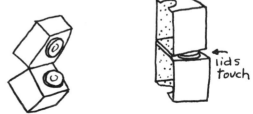

lids touch

3 Curve two strips of heavy paper to make straps for your hands. Secure the straps to the inside with tape, as shown.

4 Insert your fingers in the top strap and your thumb in the bottom strap. Open and close your hand so that the lids clink together. If you wish, add eyeballs to the top of the box and you will have a "monster clinker."

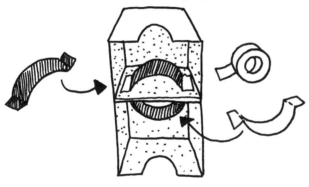

Make a Medieval Castle Theatre

Materials

a medium-sized box (The box should be lower than the height of your tubes.)

6 (or 4) long cardboard tubes from wrapping paper (If they are not available, roll tubes of heavy paper or bristol board and secure with tape.)

tempera or other paint and paint brush

2 long pieces of string

6 to 8 Popsicle sticks or long sticks toothpicks

scraps of paper and bristol board

⚠ Also: scissors, utility knife, masking tape, compass (or tool for making holes), twist-ties

1 Have an adult cut off the top and bottom of your box. Then cut off one long side of your box.

2 To make the towers, first decide whether you want a castle with four or six towers. Hold the tubes against the side of the box and mark the height of the box on your tubes. Cut up one of the tubes as far as the mark. On the opposite side of the same tube, cut the same distance. Repeat with all the tubes.

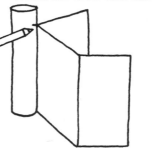
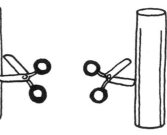

3 Slide the cut tubes over the edge of the box at the corners and ends. If you are using six tubes, slide two tubes over the middle section. Be sure to leave enough room for your drawbridge.

4 Tape the top and bottom of the tubes to the front and back of the walls.

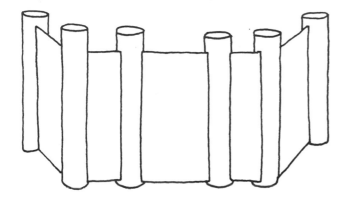

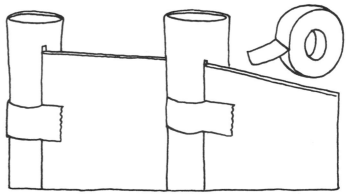

5 To make turrets, cut notches out of the towers and the walls. An easy way to do this is to cut two lines down and fold the cut section forward. Cut along the fold.

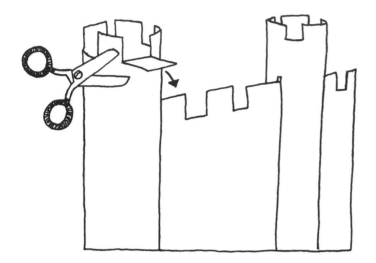

6 Using a ruler and pencil, draw your castle door in the middle section of the castle. Have an adult cut out the door with a utility knife. Save the piece — it will be your drawbridge.

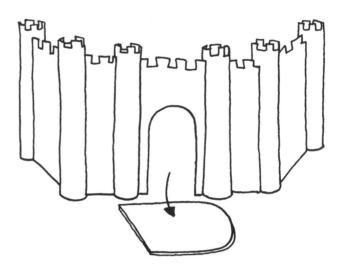

7 Paint the entire structure one colour. White or grey paint works well. Paint on stones and bricks if you like. Paint the drawbridge as well and let both dry.

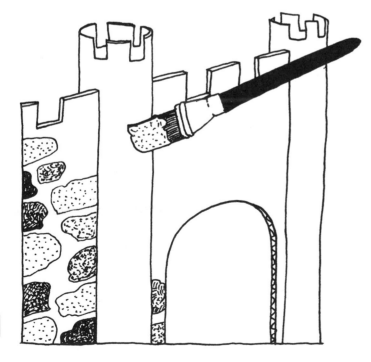

8 Make the drawbridge by punching two small holes in the bottom of the door piece you cut out. Make two holes in the walls beside the door hole. Attach the drawbridge to the doorway by sliding twist-ties through each pair of holes and twisting them at the back of the walls.

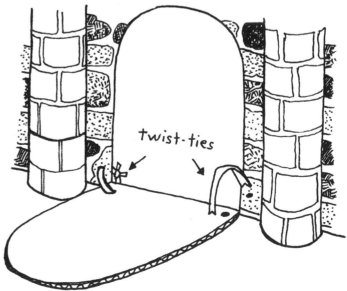

twist-ties

9 To attach string to the drawbridge, make two small holes on the top sides of the drawbridge. Pierce two holes in the wall beside the top area of the doorway. Put the strings through the holes in the drawbridge and knot them. If this is difficult, thread a needle and use thread instead of string. Put the other ends of the string through the holes in the wall. Tie large knots at the end of each string. Now you can open and close the drawbridge by pulling the strings.

Add details

To add floors to your towers, push circles of paper inside the tops of the tubes and secure with tape. Make flags with paper and toothpicks.

Make stick puppets

Make knights, horses, foot soldiers and men-at-arms out of bristol board. You could also have a Baron and a Lady. Add a tab to the bottom of each figure and secure them with tape to Popsicle sticks. Now you're ready to put on a play.

Variation

For a different kind of castle, cut a box as shown. You could make hand puppets instead of stick puppets.

Make a Shadow Theatre

Materials

a medium-sized box
tempera or other paint and paint brush
8 brass fasteners
an old white cotton sheet or white fabric
    large enough to cover the bottom of
    the box
coloured paper
black bristol board or black heavy paper
a small lamp
several metal coat hangers
pliers
Also: scissors, utility knife, masking tape

1 Cut the flaps off the top of the box.

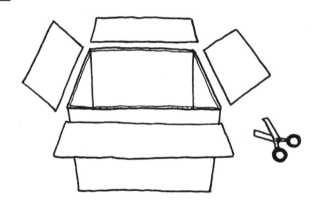

2 Turn the box on its side and draw diagonal lines on two opposite sides of the box. Then join these diagonals with a line across the top of the box and have an adult cut along all three lines.

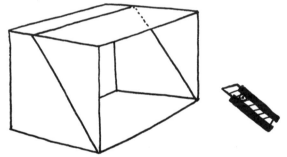

3 To make the screen frame, draw straight lines close to the edges of the bottom of the box. Have an adult cut along the lines with heavy scissors or a utility knife. (Depending on the box, it may be easier to open up the bottom flaps to do the cutting.) Secure the frame with tape.

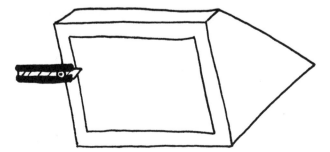

4 Paint the shadow theatre. If you wish, paint only the outside.

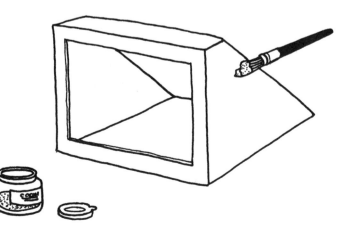

5 Make small holes in the corners and the mid-points of the frame. Insert a brass fastener through a corner hole at the front of the frame and push it through a corner of the fabric. Pull the material tight and insert brass fasteners through the frame and the fabric at the other corners and then at the mid-points. Trim off any extra fabric. (You can use frosted acetate instead of fabric if it is available.)

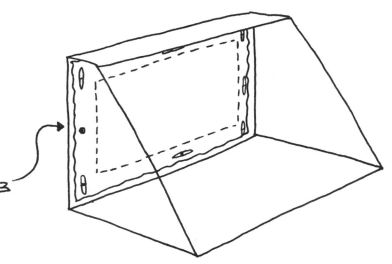

6 Trim the edges of the frame with strips of paper. Secure them with glue or masking tape. Then decorate your frame, using whatever theme you like. If you wish, add a peak to the top of the theatre and decorate it.

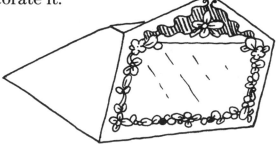

7 You can make black paper inserts for your screen. Cut out trees and bushes from black paper and attach them behind the screen to the edges of the frame.

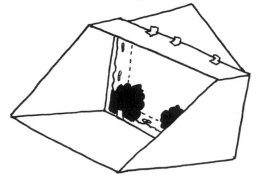

8 For the lighting, use a small table lamp and stand it in the middle back area of the screen.

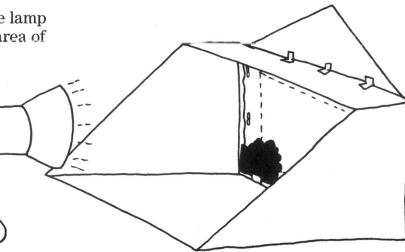

9 To make the shadow puppets, draw a rough plan of your figures, then decide which parts will move. Draw each part on black bristol board or black heavy paper and cut it out. At the joints, make holes and attach the parts together with brass fasteners.

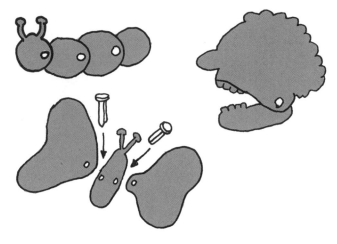

10 Have an adult help you make rods to move your puppets. Using the pliers, cut and bend coat hangers into straight rods. Bend the ends of the hangers and tape them to the back of the shadow puppets, attaching them to the parts you want to move.

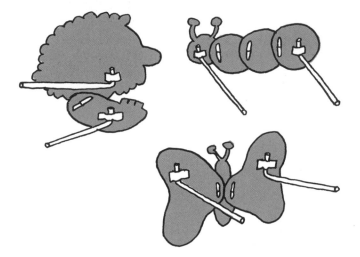

11 Practise moving your figures. If you wish, make a curtain for your theatre. You can draw it closed at the end of each act and announce the next one.

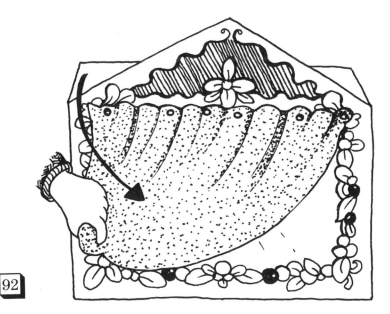

Variation

Try making theatres with a jungle theme, space theme or circus theme. Also, you can use hand shadows instead of shadow puppets.

Stages

You can make wonderful stages from boxes.
Here are some ideas!

Large Standing Stages

Flat standing stage: Open a large box and
remove the top, bottom and one side. Cut a
window in the front of the box.

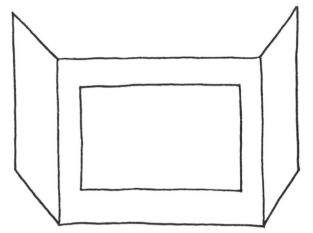

Corner stage: Use a square box. Remove
the top and bottom and cut a large window
on one corner. Cut the opposite two sides
as shown.

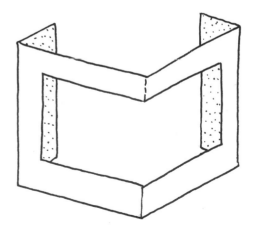

Stage with a window sill: Make a flat
standing stage (see left) but cut out only
the top half of the window. Slit down the
sides to the bottom of the window. Draw
three parallel lines on the remaining
window half. Score and fold along these
lines. Bend the sections forward, then in
towards the box. Secure the bottom of the
sill to the stage with masking tape.

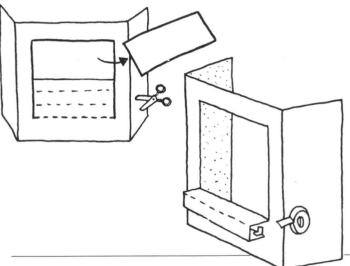

Table-top Theatres

Use the above designs with smaller boxes
to make table-top theatres.

Curtains

Double curtains: Cut two pieces of fabric, each half as wide as your theatre and 2.5 cm (1 in.) longer than your theatre is tall. On each piece of fabric, fold over 2.5 cm (1 in.) at the top and sew it in place to form a "tunnel." Thread a piece of string (a little longer than your theatre is wide) through both "tunnels," as shown. Attach the ends of the string to the top inside front of your theatre.

Single curtain that lifts: Use a piece of fabric the same size as the front of your theatre. Sew large stitches up the sides of your material using yarn or heavy thread. Attach the top of your curtain to the top inside front of your theatre. When you pull up the ends of the yarn, your curtain will lift.

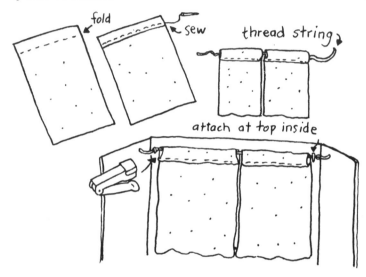

Ways to Decorate Your Theatre

Paint it.

Paint the theatre and glue on paper decorations.

Cover the theatre with paper or wallpaper.

Large Stage Sets and Props

You may have *lots* of big boxes left over from a moving day or from new appliances. What can you do with them? Why not put on a play?

Here are some ideas:

Make large movable figures

Open up boxes. Draw, colour and cut out large figures. Attach hand straps to the back of the figures. People can stand behind them and move them about the stage.

Make trees

Use a tall box, or stack and tape a number of boxes together. Cut strips of green tissue paper or cut up green garbage bags and tape them to the top of the box. Make fruit trees by adding paper apples or cherries.

To make balloon trees, tie a number of balloons together and attach them to a trunk made from a box.

Make an archway

Stack boxes to make an entrance or an archway.

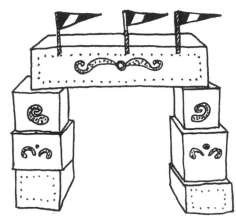

Make furniture

Make tables, chairs, stoves, refrigerators and televisions from boxes.

Make backdrops

Open up boxes and paint scenes on them to create backdrops. Change the backdrops for different scenes in your play.

Make popping boxes

Have a person hide inside a box. The person can push a stick attached to a sign or object through a hole in the box.

Make large structures

You can build a fence between boxes or hang banners between them.

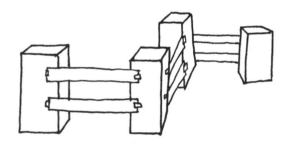

Hang boxes

You can make bird cages that hang from the ceiling or from a box tree.

Make giant box animals

Giant box animals can be backdrops or they can be large costumes.

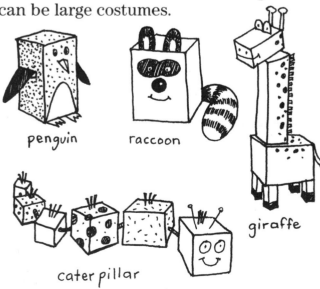

penguin

raccoon

giraffe

caterpillar

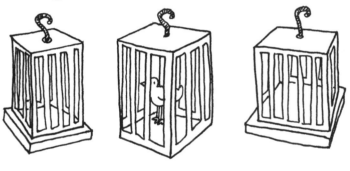

dragon   moose   rabbit

Cut into boxes

Cut into the top of large boxes to make stand-up eyes and tails.

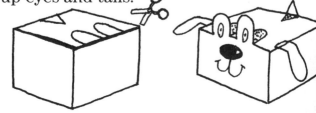